Average to All-Star

"Leaders rely on smart systems to help them lead in organizations, in the classroom, on the court, and at home. *Average to All-Star* provides an intentional three-step approach that every smart leader craves to develop our future leaders. This book will inspire you, challenge you, and encourage you to positively impact our future."

—**Mark Brand**, senior associate athletics director, media relations, Arizona State University

"When looking through the pages of the Bible, we recognize King David was an incredible leader. In Psalm 78:72, we read that David led with "integrity of heart" and "skillful hands." In *Average to All-Star*, Sharlee gives us a framework for developing young leaders that demonstrate competency and character in their leadership."

—**Kraig Cabe**, regional vice president, Fellowship of Christian Athletes

"If you want to take a master class on inspiring others, then Sharlee is the star teacher. In my four years as a college student, Sharlee has instilled a supreme level of confidence in me as a mother would her son. Sharlee's powerful messages have routinely motivated me to take on any challenge that helps me go further faster."

—**Nick Sprecher**, PepsiCo

"I would not be where I am in my career today without guidance and expertise from Sharlee. The journey she takes young leaders on is truly powerful!"

—**Riley Boots**, Anheuser-Busch

"I was fortunate enough to be mentored by Sharlee during my formative undergrad years. She consistently guided me to learn critical parts about myself that I didn't know were there. Sharlee's decades of experience equipped her to quickly identify important attributes in me (and other young leaders) and help me lean into the ways I'm gifted."

—**Brendan Gillenwater**, American Airlines

"I met Sharlee at the beginning of my professional journey, as a young student. Her ability to combine compassion, enthusiasm, and intellect is what makes her such an invaluable coach. She not only shares the tools to harness your strengths but shows you how valuable you are."

—**Eesha Patel**, Microsoft

"Sharlee Lyons is a gifted leader of leaders. When I was younger, she saw something in me that I didn't quite see in myself. She came alongside me and raised me up to be the leader I am today. Without her, I wouldn't be who I am or where I am at. She's an incredible coach, and I know that this book will provide so much insight to other emerging leaders across the globe!"

—**Tanner Watkins**, Northview Church

"Sharlee Lyons has a well-earned reputation of excellence and expertise in regard to developing leaders. No one understands better than Sharlee the process of going from average to All-Star and all of the steps, hurdles, and support needed to do so. Sharlee's method of engagement has proven results with student leaders and beyond."

—**Raven Scott**, founder of The Training Ground

"I cannot think of someone who is more qualified to share insights on how to become a better leader than Sharlee! She has decades of hands-on experience working with young leaders and helping them reach their potential. I personally benefited tremendously from Sharlee's teaching and her passion in leadership, and I can't wait to see more people get to learn and grow their leadership skills following her system!"
—**Terrence Li**, senior technology risk consultant for one of the "Big Four" accounting firms

"Sharlee has always helped young leaders discover their leadership potential by offering opportunities and resources for them to grow. Sharlee introduced me to several of my most memorable undergraduate leadership experiences, and it was always reassuring to know that I could always count on her wise advice whenever I encountered a roadblock. If it wasn't for all the opportunities that Sharlee encouraged me to explore, I could still be on the path trying to find the challenge-seeking, objective thinking, ambitious, and determined individual that I am today."
—**Xintong (Ruby) Zheng**

"There is a gap between information and wisdom that can often only be bridged by real-life experience. What Sharlee shares in this resource is more than just ideas or theory; it is real-life wisdom she's lived out serving, leading, and empowering others to succeed. She brings a unique and different perspective, and anyone who takes her words to heart will benefit."
—**JT Thoms**, host and creator of REMARKable Recruitment

"Sharlee is a leader who shares advice and actively listens. These strengths and her decades of experience make her an expert on how to cultivate the next generation of leadership."

—**Grace In**, consultant at one of the "Big Four" consulting firms

> Tom —
> Thanks for impacting so many all-stars in your work & career.
> ♥ Sharlee

Average to All-Star

Equipping Young Leaders to Start Strong *and Go Further Faster*

Sharlee Lyons

Foreword by Dr. Tim Elmore

Niche Pressworks

Average to All-Star

Copyright © 2022 by Sharlee Lyons

All rights reserved. No part of this book may be used or reproduced in any manner whatsoever without prior written consent of the author, except as provided by the United States of America copyright law.

Some names and details have been changed to protect the privacy of the individuals involved.

While the author has made every effort to provide accurate internet addresses at the time of publication, neither the publisher nor the author assumes any responsibility for errors or changes that occur after publication. Further, the publisher does not have control over and does not assume any responsibility for author or third-party websites or their content.

The author and publisher specifically disclaim liability, loss, or risk, personal or otherwise, which is incurred as a consequence, directly or indirectly, of the use or application of any of the contents of this book.

For permission to reprint portions of this content or bulk purchases, contact sharlee@sharleelyons.com.

978-1-952654-48-0 Paperback
978-1-952654-49-7 eBook
978-1-952654-53-4 Hardback

Published by Niche Pressworks; http://NichePressworks.com

Indianapolis, IN

The views expressed herein are solely those of the author and do not necessarily reflect the views of the publisher.

Acknowledgements

To the God of the universe who knit me together in my mother's womb, I will praise you because I am fearfully and wonderfully made. And I pray that I may be an encouragement to others to see themselves in the same fashion.

To those who chose me and have spoken life into me, I am eternally grateful. There are too many of you to count; believe me, I tried. You enrich my life.

To my husband, Todd, thanks for encouraging me to follow my calling and chase my dreams.

To Noah and Sarah, God gave you life and breath and has a purpose for you. May your lives be filled with finding and fulfilling that purpose and with many who help you along the way. I'm happy He chose you as mine.

Contents

Foreword xiii

INTRODUCTION: CHANGING A LIFE 1

    The Power of Mentorship 3
    Twelve Reasons Coaches and Mentors Are Important ... 5
    The Art of Leadership Development 6
    Self-Assessment: What Are Your Personal Mentoring Challenges? 7
    Chosen to Be Extraordinary 10
    A Leadership Shortage Looms 11
    The Keys to Good Mentorship 15
    The Power of Intention 16
    Mindset Tip: Do the First Push-Up 16
    The 3D System: From Average to All-Star 18

STEP 1: DISCOVER 21

1. **OBSERVE** 23
    Observing with Intention:
        Coaches and Crystal Balls 25
    Find Your 'Why' 27
    The Power of Sociograms 29
    Your Observational Superpowers 32
    Find the True Leaders 34
    Exercise: Vision and Action 37
    Exercise: Find Your 'Bucket List' of Chosen Leaders ... 39

x AVERAGE TO ALL-STAR

2. **ACKNOWLEDGE**	**45**
What It Means to Be Chosen	45
Speaking into Emerging Leaders	48
Exercise: Acknowledge One of Your Chosen	51
3. **EVALUATE**	**53**
Behaviors Point to Passion	53
Observational Assessment:	
The Three Spheres of Leadership	56
Take a Strengths Inventory	59
Plug the Holes	61
Useful Assessment Tools	64
Exercise: The Three Spheres Assessment	68

STEP 2: DEVELOP   73

4. **EXPECT**	**75**
Developing through Expectations	77
The Call to Leadership	83
Exercise: Define Your Chosen's Calling	89
5. **PLAN**	**95**
Set and Achieve Expectations Together	95
Base the Plan on Your Chosen's Values	96
A Good Plan Creates Motivation	98
Steps to Create a Development Action Plan	99
Exercise: Create an Action Plan for Your Chosen	103
6. **GUIDE**	**107**
The Role of a Guide	111
The Top Ten Mistakes Coaches and Mentors Make	114
Keeping Your Mentee (and You!) Motivated	120
Did I Do Something Wrong?	122

CONTENTS   xi

    What If I Have to End the Relationship?   124
    Exercise: Create a Coaching Framework
    for Working with Your Mentee   126

STEP 3: DEPLOY   **129**

7. **INSTILL**   **131**
    The Drive for Excellence   132
    Teaching the Excellence Mindset   134
    Ways to Develop Excellence   136
    Beware of Dwelling on Mistakes   143
    Developing Confidence and Deploying Excellence   145
    Exercise: Help Your Mentee Internalize Excellence and Gain
    Confidence   146

8. **STRATEGIZE**   **149**
    Deployment Strategy vs. Development Plan   153
    The Other Side of the Equation: Needs   157
    Exercise: Do a T Model for Your Chosen   159

9. **ADAPT**   **161**
    Adapting on the Fly   163
    Agility on a Grander Leadership Scale   164
    The Key to Agility   166
    Self-Leadership   167
    Exercise: Be an Example of Agility   169

10. **WHAT'S NEXT?**   **171**
    It's Time to Act   172
    Circle of Impact   173

Thank You   **175**
About the Author   **177**

Foreword

An excellent mentor and coach can take on many roles. They are the friend sipping a latte with you at a coffee shop, offering a listening ear and wise counsel. They are the seasoned co-worker and leader pulling you aside at the water cooler to help you coach someone about fixing a mistake. They are the concerned parent, not allowing you to settle for less than your best. They are the coach, assessing your technical mistakes and giving you a plan for addressing them. And they are the cheerleader, giving you that extra push of support and motivation to hurdle over the next biggest challenge.

I have known Sharlee Lyons for several years now, having first worked with her as she used the Habitudes curriculum to serve the student leaders at Purdue University and to design a mentoring program for the Krannert School of Management. She went on to become a master consultant with my organization, Growing Leaders. She's a well-rounded mentor and coach, as she's also a Gallup Certified Strengths Coach, a Fascinate Certified Advisor, and is certified by the International Coaches Federation. As we became better acquainted, I observed her as a committed professional, wife, and mother. She is warm. She is bright. She is discerning.

Most of all, she is the friend, the experienced leader, the cheerleader—all of the facets that make up an excellent coach and mentor, and more. And now, she wants to equip you for the same excellence, through the pages of this book.

As you progress through the pages of *Average to All-Star*, she will engage you in a conversation about your growth and success that transfers into the growth and success of our youngest generations. You'll encounter steps and challenges in your own growth as you prepare to grow future leaders.

Prepare for some epiphanies. Get ready to act.

She honestly believes in you as you lift your Chosen out of the average mindset and into All-Star mentality and performance. She will exhort you to set loftier goals and to see higher visions. She will do her best to prepare and motivate you to do your best so that you can do the same for your own mentees.

And frankly, the world needs more excellent mentors and coaches.

Sharlee passionately believes there is **so much more** to attain than an average life. And so do I. However, neither of us believes the difference between average and All-Star is about talent or IQ. We believe it's about discovering, developing, and deploying whatever it is that's inside you and your Chosen.

In other words, it's about you.

Because with the right intention, tools, and planning, anyone can do those vital things.

This book isn't merely a bunch of theories from an academic. The content was forged from real-life experiences with young adults who at one point felt they were merely "average." Sharlee would not let them settle for mediocre when she saw something more inside. And she wants you to harness that same vision, passion, and purpose in your own way, too.

If you don't want to settle for an average life and instead want to pursue an All-Star life for yourself and others, this book could be just the tool you need. Why not start now?

Tim Elmore
Founder and CEO
Growing Leaders

"The growth and development of others is the highest calling of leadership."

—HARVEY S. FIRESTONE

INTRODUCTION

Changing a Life

"I don't EVER want to do that again, and I don't know what to tell my parents," Caitlin told me as she stood in my office, where she had briefly dropped by to see me.

She had just returned to campus from her summer internship. All I had done was ask how her summer had been, yet I could already tell something was wrong—she was on the verge of tears.

For a moment, all she could do was shake her head. If she spoke, the tears would come.

She obviously needed immediate attention. Checking the schedule on my phone, I saw with relief that I had some time to devote to her. To get her out of the building and away from others she knew who might see her looming tears, I whisked her away to a coffee shop that was off the beaten path and had outdoor seating.

As we sat in the warm sunshine of early fall, she fidgeted, seeming ready to explode from the pent-up stress and emotions. But finally, she opened up.

The problem, it turned out, was her summer internship. She was a top-tier student in the undergraduate management program and had landed her internship at a Fortune 50 company. She was on the fast track to an accomplished corporate career. But despite being very capable, she had found the experience miserable. Now, she wondered what she was going to do. She had thought she had a plan for herself—one her parents stood solidly behind. What now?

I knew I had to let her work through the explanation and, more importantly, her emotions. I listened for quite some time until she got everything out.

After she finally took a deep breath of relief, we sat in silence for what seemed an eternity, even though it was only for about thirty seconds. Finally, I asked, "What do YOU really want to do, Caitlin?"

She responded with a long explanation of what her parents wanted and expected of her.

When she finished, I asked again, "What do YOU really want, Caitlin?"

She sat back in her chair, took a big drink of her now-cooled coffee, and said, "What I really want is to own my own fashion boutique where I can make women feel beautiful and empowered to cultivate joy around themselves."

Wow. It was articulate, succinct, and so well-rehearsed. She had obviously been thinking about this for a long time.

We talked about steps she would need to take if she really wanted to pursue her own boutique—and how she would have to overcome her parents' expectations, perceived or otherwise, that she go into a corporate career. She would have to be brave in communicating her plan and getting their buy-in.

As we talked, she put together steps to pursue her dream.

Initially, she did have to deal with her parents' opposition and uncertainty, but after several coaching sessions with me, she eventually won their support, and they even gave her a few thousand dollars to purchase a plane ticket to a show where she could purchase inventory.

She was encouraged that her mother attended the show with her and was starting to buy into and get excited about her boutique idea. Our work together, combined with Caitlin's determination to succeed, was paying off.

Caitlin opened her online boutique about six months later and ran it while attending school and pursuing other development opportunities that would support her dream. She completed an internship I had suggested that focused on leadership development. That internship was a huge growth experience for her as well. We had worked together to develop a strong leadership foundation that supported her dream.

She owned her boutique for several years before taking on a full-time position at a dynamic women's brand that has revolutionized its industry. And with the recent sale of the majority of the company, the CEO gifted Caitlin and her colleagues with two first-class plane tickets to anywhere in the world, along with $10,000.

The Power of Mentorship

What if Caitlin hadn't had a mentor to talk to? What if she hadn't been guided to live her own authentic values and her real potential and had decided instead to just "hunker down and get through it" and figure it out later?

What if "later" never came, and she stayed in a career she didn't like?

What if thousands—even millions—of young potential leaders were doing exactly that—living lives where their true authenticity and potential never shine through?

It's a terrible thought—but it's happening every day.

The question is, why?

Why Don't More People Live Their True Potential?

Mentors choose to coach people in whom they see potential. John Maxwell sums up the qualities of potential well, saying, "[Potential] looks forward with optimism. It promises success. It implies fulfillment. It hints at extraordinary. It believes in possibilities. Potential is exciting."[1]

Unfulfilled potential, on the other hand, looks backward with regret. It produces mediocrity instead of excellence. It implies no true intention. And it shows a lack of accountability.

Achievement creates confidence, leading to more achievement. Unfulfilled potential deflates and downright saddens a person and leads to less and less achievement—even to giving up entirely.

If unfulfilled potential is so depressing, why does it even happen? Why can't we avoid it?

There are many complex psychological reasons, but one underlying fact is simple enough: we get what we expect.

If we expect failure, we get failure. If we expect average, we get average. If we expect extraordinary, we get extraordinary. And if no one expects anything of us, or we aren't sure what to expect of ourselves, we have nothing to build from to improve. If we don't know what to expect, and if we don't know how to understand whether we're fulfilling our potential or what to do when we're not, where do we go?

What's the answer?

---

1   John Maxwell, *The 15 Invaluable Laws of Growth* (New York: Hachette Book Group, 2012).

It's simple: to help us discover and live our true potential, we need coaches and mentors.

Twelve Reasons Coaches and Mentors Are Important[2]

1. **Mentors support growth.** They encourage and enable another person's professional and personal development.

2. **Mentors serve as a source of knowledge.** They can provide specific insights and information that enable mentees' success.

3. **Mentors can help set goals.** They can help their mentees set personal and professional development goals.

4. **Mentors can maintain accountability.** They help hold their mentees accountable to their own goals.

5. **Mentors offer encouragement.** They can encourage and motivate their mentees to keep moving forward despite their challenges.

6. **Mentors make connections.** They can help build their mentees' professional networks.

7. **Mentors are willing to listen.** They can provide unbiased advice or opinions using their relevant knowledge and experience.

8. **Mentors serve as trusted allies.** They have the mentee's best interest in mind and provide accurate and honest guidance.

---

[2] "24 Reasons Why Mentorship is Important," Indeed, February 22, 2021, https://www.indeed.com/career-advice/career-development/why-is-a-mentor-important/.

9. **Mentors can offer constructive feedback.** They give honest feedback that can identify weaknesses and advise on ways to improve.

10. **Mentors provide guidelines.** They can help set professional expectations.

11. **Mentors have relevant experience.** They have a strong understanding of professional situations and related goals.

12. **Mentors are a free resource.** They genuinely want to help others and establish an authentic connection above and beyond a business-client paid relationship.

The Art of Leadership Development

> "Successful leaders realize that true leaders don't create more followers; they create more leaders."
> —TOM PETERS

Smart leaders know that developing others' potential gives greater power to the whole organization, enabling it to better meet its goals. Not only that, but these resulting new leaders go beyond the organization to make the world a better place through all their actions.

"All right," you say, "but what if I'm not a leader?"

"Really?" I will respond. "Who says you're not?"

What?

Yes—it's time to think outside the box.

One of the reasons more people don't mentor others is because many people don't see themselves as qualified or worthy to help guide others in their lives. Or they just don't know how, and they're afraid to make a mistake. No one wants to mess up and negatively affect someone else's life. And then there are all the other reasons—it's hard to find the time to be engaged with another person's life, or it's difficult to break the ice and create a comfortable mentoring relationship. No one wants to be seen as "butting in" or inserting themselves where they don't belong.

If you're reading this book, you probably want to make a difference, and if you're a normal person, you probably also have at least one of the qualms I just listed. However, the need for mentors and coaches today is greater than it's ever been—and if we really want to see our future generations succeed, it's time to start thinking about how to get past these obstacles and find innovative ways to become part of the solutions. They need all of us—and we need them.

And I'm here to tell you that there are solutions—lots of them! And despite what you might believe, they aren't especially complicated, nor do they take up a lot of your time.

However, before you start reading about solutions, let's work together to define your own particular "problem" so you can figure out where to concentrate your own efforts.

Self-Assessment: What Are Your Personal Mentoring Challenges?

It's time for a moment of honest self-reflection: where are you in the "mentoring mix"? Check any that apply:

- ☐ I consistently tap others' potential and help them shape their skills to become leaders. Those I've mentored/coached have gone on to do great things in their fields/careers/lives. However, there's always more to learn, and I like to hear new ideas for increasing my ability to help others.

☐ I do all right guiding some people, but I'm not always sure what to do/say, and I don't always know how to approach those I see who need some guidance. I need to learn some approaches that will increase my confidence.

☐ I've tried to help some people, but I don't feel they listen, and what I say doesn't seem to matter. It's frustrating to put time toward others but not see it go toward a positive result. I need to find ways to increase my effectiveness.

☐ I want to help make a difference in others' lives, but I haven't done much because I don't know how to go about it, and I don't know what I have to offer them. Plus, I'm afraid I'll say/do the wrong thing. I don't feel I'm qualified to help others. I need to understand more about how I could help and to gain confidence that I can make a positive difference in a way I'm comfortable with.

☐ I want to help make a difference in others' lives, but it seems like a challenging task when I'm already overwhelmed with other things in my own life. I don't feel I have time for such a big commitment. I need some idea of what I'm getting myself into and ways to be effective so that I don't feel like I'm in over my head.

If any of the assessment selections from 2–5 resonate with you, you're not alone. And even if I didn't hit on your own specific situation in the preceding descriptions, there is probably another person who has the same challenges you do. However, challenges are made to be overcome. No matter what the situation is, you can find a solution—whether it's looking at things from a different perspective, finding a system that works, or learning a new skill.

So: are you ready to break the cycle and help others achieve their best potential? If so, let's first clear things up with some definitions.

Leadership = Influence = YOU
"The key to successful leadership today is influence, not authority."
—KENNETH BLANCHARD

Most people think of a leader as an authority. However, there are different kinds of leaders and authorities—and different kinds of mentors and mentoring relationships. We'll explore those further later in the book, but for now, let's get one thing straight: what does the term "leader" even mean?

For me, "influence" and "leadership" are synonymous. However, people from different backgrounds and age groups often define or see things differently—or think they do, even when they don't. For instance, if you ask someone from Gen Z who their generation's leaders are, they may look at you with a blank stare, but if you ask them who the "influencers" are, they will rattle a handful off before you can blink. They are just thinking in different words, but they come to the same thing. When I'm engaging with the younger set, I try to use the term "influencer" instead of "leader" so they can relate better to what I'm saying, but the two terms are actually interchangeable to me.

The *Oxford English Dictionary Online* defines influence as "the capacity to have an effect on the character, development, or behavior of someone or something," or in verb form, "to affect or change someone or something in an indirect but usually important way."[3]

---

3 Oxford English Dictionary Online, s.v. "influence," accessed March 25, 2022, https://www.google.com/search?client=firefox-b-1-d&q=definition+influence

Many mentors may not be the traditional idea of "leaders" defined as "people in roles of organizational authority," but that doesn't mean they aren't qualified to help guide someone. They can still have some type of influence within the person's life.

It's also important to note that influencers' effects can be positive or negative. Even those with negative influence are leaders. In the lives of some young people, if the negative influencers outweigh the positive ones, the person is in much greater danger of either falling short of his or her potential or using it in destructive ways. The more positive influencers we have who are willing and able to truly help others, the less influence the negative leaders will have—they will be outnumbered and outmatched.

Chosen to Be Extraordinary

So. What do mentors do? They choose to help others be extraordinary...which in itself is also extraordinary.

When my brothers and I were growing up, one of my mom's favorite quotes was, "It takes so little to be above average."

Pro Football Hall of Fame coach Jimmy Johnson took my mom's philosophy up a notch: "The difference between ordinary and extraordinary is the little extra."

They're both absolutely right. Even just a little thought, effort, and understanding in the right places can change someone's performance from average to extraordinary.

No one is born with average *potential*—the key is what they do with it. To me, Psalm 139 says it beautifully when it claims that we are "fearfully and wonderfully made."[4] You were chosen

---

4   Ps. 139:14 *Life Application Bible New International Version* (Carol Stream, IL: Tyndale House Publishers, Inc., 1990)

by God and made to be above average! Whether you embrace scripture or not, it is easy to note that we all have special gifts, talents, and abilities. There is no other person knit together quite like you.

Everyone has something to offer to others. That includes you. If you have knowledge, experience, or understanding that can benefit another person, you are an actual or potential influencer. Your choices determine whether your influence is average or extraordinary. So, if you are looking around the world and see young people who seem to have lost their way, don't wait for someone else to help them.

You are the someone else.

You can *choose yourself* to be extraordinary so that you can help them become extraordinary.

If you're feeling a little afraid of that kind of expectation, don't worry. I'm not going to expect a lot of you and then leave you to figure it all out on your own. I've been doing this a long time, and I can give you a jump-start in helping others. Through this book, I will mentor you, just as you would like to mentor others. And believe me, they need you.

A Leadership Shortage Looms

I believe our youngest generations are some of the most talented in history. But we may not be teaching them all the skills they need to succeed in life. And we aren't giving many of them the time to develop the leadership muscle they need to lead us into the future.

Our future leaders are lacking in four key areas:

1. **Numbers.** There are too few young leaders to meet current and future demands.

Baby boomers are entering retirement age at a rate of 10,000 per day.[5] In the third quarter of 2020 alone, 25.4 million more boomers retired than in the entire year of 2011.[6] There aren't enough Gen Xers to fill their leadership and other roles. Meanwhile, studies predict that in just five years, millennials will amount to about 75 percent of the global workforce. Yet a whopping 63 percent of millennials currently feel their workplaces aren't helping them develop their leadership skills well enough.[7] With 75 million baby boomers retiring sooner or later (and right now, it's sooner), it's clear that employers will need a strong workforce plan for replacing exiting leaders. If employers aren't developing their millennials, who will fill the leadership gap?

2. **Skill.** Young leaders aren't getting the skills they need as quickly as they need them.

    One problem is simply the lack of sufficient mentoring and support. Millennials say they crave feedback, but only 19 percent feel they are receiving feedback from their managers, and only 17 percent feel the feedback is meaningful.[8]

    But multiple other factors have delayed or impaired our young leaders' opportunities to learn.

    For instance, many millennials who graduated and entered tough job markets in the past were forced to take positions that didn't reflect their authentic values, personal missions, or skills.

---

5   PushFar. "Mentoring Statistics in 2022. Everything You Need to Know," accessed April 20, 2022, https://www.pushfar.com/article/mentoring-statistics-everything-you-need-to-know/.

6   PushFar, April 20, 2022.

7   PushFar, April 20, 2022.

8   Ibid.

As a result, many are choosing to change positions—and even fields—to new ones that resonate better with them. I believe this trend will continue, creating a need for more learning as they work to gain experience in the new field.

Labor demands, in general, are creating a shorter timespan for young leaders to prepare for their leadership responsibilities. Organizations generally show extended patience in cases of less seasoned leaders, but today's emergent leaders are not taking full advantage of those opportunities.

The COVID-19 pandemic set off massive changes that we will continue to feel for years to come. I'm not sure we even know the true impact yet. Lockdowns and limitations in interaction certainly limited opportunities for young leaders' growth and development in many regions for months and years.

Moreover, as the post-pandemic shift to greater numbers of people working remotely continues, younger leaders will have less interpersonal access to others on a daily basis. They are losing opportunities to develop close relationships with seasoned leaders and skill and knowledge area experts who can provide more in-depth feedback as they work.

According to *Harvard Business Review*, as mentoring relationships shift to virtual and email/text formats that limit the day-to-day interpersonal "mentor of the moment" opportunities, mentors will need to ensure they intentionally create the opportunities that previously resulted naturally, just from being in the same onsite environment.[9]

---

9   Ellen A. Enscher, W. Brad Johnson, & David G. Smith, "How to Mentor in a Remote Workplace," March 22, 2022, *Harvard Business Review*, accessed at https://hbr.org/2022/03/how-to-mentor-in-a-remote-workplace.

3. **Maturity.** Our emerging leaders are not emotionally mature and are suffering from social and emotional issues.

    These generations have delayed learning and social-emotional development. Research shows that people's brains don't reach adulthood until age 30.[10]

    Members of Generation Z are significantly more likely (27 percent) than other generations, including millennials (15 percent) and Gen Xers (13 percent), to report their mental health as fair or poor, according to a survey conducted on behalf of the American Psychological Association. Not surprisingly, America's younger generations are also more likely to have received treatment or therapy from a mental health professional: 37 percent of Generation Z and 35 percent of millennials have reported doing so compared to just 26 percent of Gen Xers and 22 percent of baby boomers.[11]

4. **Motivation.** They are not engaged.

    Only 29 percent of millennials report feeling engaged at work.[12] And, with the current labor shortage, they don't have to stay stuck in a job they don't like. That should give HR departments concern, especially when four out of ten workers who don't have mentors say they've considered quitting their job in the past three months.[13]

---

[10] Melissa Matthews, "People's Brains Don't Reach Adulthood Until Age 30, Study Finds" Men's Health.com. March 19, 2019, https://www.menshealth.com/health/a26868313/when-does-your-brain-fully-mature/.

[11] Annie E. Casey Foundation, "Generation Z and Mental Health," updated October 16, 2021, https://www.aecf.org/blog/generation-z-and-mental-health.

[12] Annie E. Casey Foundation, "What the Statistics Say about Generation Z"; *Casey Connects*; November 13, 2020; https://www.aecf.org/blog/generation-z-statistics

[13] Ibid.

And as mentioned previously in the "skills" concern, many younger leaders had to go into jobs that were not an ideal fit. In these cases, their situation may be negatively affecting their motivation.

As their mentors, we are responsible for helping young leaders to course correct. We cannot leave them in this situation. We are teetering on a cliff with a huge chasm of leadership deficiency before us. We must choose to do something now.

We can't afford to wait another second to help our future leaders develop the skills and experience they need to take society through the challenges we face as we continue to evolve. Our future depends on our taking action now!

The Keys to Good Mentorship

When Caitlin needed help in her crisis, I didn't hesitate. I wasn't worried about what to say or do. With more than twenty years of experience mentoring and developing teams and individuals in many sectors, I knew how to approach the situation.

I didn't develop that confidence overnight, however. I've observed good coaches and mentors throughout my life, and I've noted that their skills all boil down to having two simple things:

1. **Clear intention about why they want to help others and what they want to help with.**
2. **A flexible, proven system that guides their actions.**

One of the goals of this book is to give you some tools to develop both of these in your own way, so you can effectively apply your own skills and strengths to help others.

The Power of Intention

"Intention is one of the most powerful forces there is."
—BRENNA YOVANFF

Intention must infuse the entire process of developing leaders. In developing others' potential, you must be committed and clear about why you want to develop others, whom you want to develop, and what aspects you want to develop.

Are you continually looking for potential in others? Are you committed to developing it? When you're really committed, you don't allow obstacles to hinder you—you find innovative ways to overcome them. If you're not committed, why?

Being intentional is more than just having a desire to do something. Intention requires setting specific, clear goals that create a different level of awareness and a different mindset, which lead to different actions. You're always operating in this mindset, even in the background. When you've done it enough, you learn to quickly see and assess others' potential and respond in the moment.

Mentoring doesn't have to be a long, involved process—when you learn to think like a mentor or coach, it eventually just comes naturally.

Throughout this book, I'll give you some tips for creating solid intention that will help you develop your awareness and drive your actions when those around you need help.

Mindset Tip: Do the First Push-Up

"Every journey begins with a single step."
—MAYA ANGELOU

When something seems impossible, sometimes you have to break it down into smaller pieces. It goes back to that old saying, "How do you eat an elephant? One bite at a time."

At fourteen, my daughter, Sarah, aspired to be part of the Miss America Organization and take part in a local competition. She had watched her mentor, Katie, build herself as an empowered young woman within this organization.

However, one thing stood in Sarah's way: in the competition, each contestant must perform a fitness routine that includes doing push-ups. That silly push-up was the only thing holding Sarah back from the entire competition. It wreaked havoc with her confidence and kept her from taking the first step toward her dream.

One day, driving home from baton practice, we talked about how she might overcome this barrier. She made a plan to do a set of two push-ups before bed every night and again when she got up in the morning. Within the first two weeks, she could do four push-ups per set, and at six weeks in, she got up to eight.

When I asked if it had been hard, she replied, "It wasn't hard, and it really didn't even take a lot of time. I just had to take small steps and be intentional about it." Bingo! And now the girl is doing LEGIT push-ups and was able to win her first competition.

It would have been unreasonable for Sarah to expect herself to suddenly be able to do fifty push-ups when she couldn't do one. But with intention, she created a clear plan, broke the task into manageable steps to build on over time, and took action. Suddenly, what seemed impossible became simple.

That's what we're going to do through this book.

The 3D System: From Average to All-Star

Mentoring is no different from any other process—if you have a system that works, it simplifies success in every part of the process. Though we may not have a quick fix for our looming leadership gap, a good system can help us solve the problem much more quickly and effectively than we could without one.

Do you have a system for developing your mentees? Who are your current "Chosen"? If you can't identify any, let's get to work! Even if you do have a system, you might learn some new tips. And you may even spot people you wouldn't have previously recognized as having potential.

Three little words can make such a huge difference: Discover. Develop. Deploy.

It's a simple system, but it works.

Step 1: Discover

How do you identify those with real potential? How do you know you're not missing anyone? This step uses an intentional process to help you discover those hidden future leaders all around you. You will learn to observe the people around you with intention, pinpointing those who influence. You will create a potential list of mentees and then, based on several criteria, choose those whom you'll mentor. You'll also learn how to communicate to get them on board.

Step 2: Develop

In this stage, the "aha" moments happen. Based on your own skills and expertise and the interests and focus areas of those whom you want to mentor, you'll create a list of the general leadership competencies that you want to develop in each of your Chosen. This will include their "need to knows" and their "good to knows." Then you'll assess each person's present abilities in those competencies. You and each of your Chosen will then create a development plan to improve and build their leadership competencies, focusing on a couple at a time. Finally, the Develop stage also includes you—as you coach your mentees, you yourself will improve your leadership coaching abilities and gain experience that will help your Chosen for many years to come.

Step 3: Deploy

Watching your budding young leaders make a positive difference can be exciting. In this step, you will walk your Chosen through a strategic leadership deployment process that makes sense within his or her values and goals and has lasting impact. You will help your Chosen create agility in their leadership, which will help them start strong and go further faster.

Read on to learn the details of the above steps so that you can take your mentorship and your mentees' abilities from average to All-Star.

"The purpose of life is to discover your gift. The work of life is to develop it. The meaning of life is to give your gift away."

—DAVID VISCOTT

STEP 1

DISCOVER

CHAPTER 1

Observe

> "Paying attention to the world around you will help you develop the extraordinary capacity to look at mundane things and see the miraculous."
>
> —MICHAEL MICHALKO

One young woman, whom I'll call Stephanie, had a lot of passion for her chosen field. However, it was a fairly new technical field, and there wasn't much training or certification available. She was doing very well in her career and was concerned about the lack of opportunity for others to learn. She observed that not only did some of her friends need to find viable careers, but they also had the potential to succeed in her field, too. Since they had nowhere to go for formal training, she offered to teach them herself, out of her own home. Several accepted and went on to take lucrative new positions as well. Eventually, this situation evolved into Stephanie creating an entire formal training facility and program and helping her state develop certification techniques for the budding new industry.

Stephanie's situation developed organically because not only did she love her work, but she also wanted to help her friends succeed, too. Due to her positive focus, many bright young people who were previously struggling are now able to have their own lucrative careers in the field. Some even serve as instructors in the training program, too. She has changed many people's lives for the better—yet she would never have imagined in high school that she would ever have gone on to do what she did. She didn't even like traditional school and wasn't a great student. Yet once she got into the right career, everything clicked into place for her.

As with Stephanie's story, the most powerful mentorships often happen informally. They occur when the mentor has a keen interest in not only finding new mentees but also in investing time and energy in them—sometimes with amazing outcomes. The relationship happens organically—mentor and mentee begin to meet, discuss, and explore, and mutual gratifications encourage an ongoing relationship. It's a win-win—the mentee grows in knowledge, and the mentor feels rewarded by giving back and seeing the mentee grow.

The greater your intention, the more you will notice and create these natural opportunities. When you have the intention to find potential in others, you start seeing through those filters. Suddenly, you notice things you otherwise wouldn't. When you're looking for something, you naturally find a lot more of it. The opportunities that open are still organic and informal—it's just that now, not only do they seem to occur more often, but you also generally know how to make the most of them. It doesn't feel like "work." It is energizing and fun for both you and your mentees.

Observing with Intention: Coaches and Crystal Balls

"To acquire knowledge, one must study, but to acquire wisdom, one must observe and understand."
—MARILYN VOS SAVANT

I love to observe people.

Often, they catch me watching them. Since I don't want to creep them out, the first time a person catches me looking at them, I look away quickly and hope they haven't figured me out. The second time, I've learned to give them a friendly smile that says, "I see you." Then they know I'm looking at them but in a non-threatening way. The third time, I know I have to say something. I usually make a general observation, briefly explain my life's work of developing leaders, and then compliment a leadership behavior of theirs I've seen and offer encouragement to spread more of that goodness into our world.

My favorite place to people-watch is in schools and at extracurricular activities such as sporting events. School-aged children are my favorite age group to observe because that's the age when they are just starting to show their true leadership potential. Unless my son or daughter is playing, I generally try to be a "fly on the wall" or sit high in the bleachers, so I can get a bird's-eye view in the gym, stadium, or auditorium where I can watch groups of people interact.

Any setting creates an opportunity to make a difference, however small, with just a word or an affirmation. Observing with intention expands your influence outside your general everyday circle into areas you wouldn't think of otherwise. And trust me, it doesn't have to be creepy. Almost everyone enjoys meeting new people who appreciate them.

The 'Crystal Ball' Effect

When coaches and mentors truly develop their own mentoring capabilities, they can see where their Chosen will be in two days, two weeks, and two years. This is a quality I call the "Crystal Ball" ability.

Crystal balls have appeared in fairytales for many generations. The stories usually involve a person being able to look into a globe of crystal and see the future or events that are happening far away. The concept has spread to movies and other pop-cultural references. The large technology company Oracle named its leading spreadsheet software "Crystal Ball" because it assists in predictive modeling, forecasting, simulation, and optimization—in other words, predicting the future.

To me, coaches and mentors seemed to do all of that intuitively, without thinking about it. It always seemed like a natural, God-given superpower.

But is it?

Maybe for some, but not necessarily all. Some gifts are natural—but others come with practice—and, of course, intention.

As I've already mentioned, when you intend to spot potential, your perspective shifts. You are able to mine potential and forecast ability based on existing skills, character, and the psychology of your young leaders. With your "superpower" and your experience, you can predict outcomes, too.

You might already be able to easily tell who has potential. Maybe you can spot those people from a mile away—or in my case, the cheap seats in the bleachers.

But if you feel you don't quite know how yet, don't worry. Keep watching. Take notes on what you notice. Learn to recognize patterns of behavior that lead to positive outcomes. Suddenly, you'll realize one day that you, too, have your own unique Crystal Ball that can pinpoint potential and see where it could be in the future.

All it takes is doing the equivalent of Sarah's first push-up. Break it into manageable parts, and it becomes simple.

Find Your 'Why'

As I've mentioned, intention is your "why." It drives everything about how you observe others.

Great coaches and people who have had the greatest impact live intentionally. You know them. They are the ones you can't wait to see and talk to. They are the ones you tell others about. They are the ones at whose funerals you willingly wait in line for hours to pay your respects.

They are the ones who chose you.

They had the goal to help you become extraordinary, and they worked to achieve that through their particular role in your life.

Vision Leads to Action

In leadership, we talk about "vision," which is simply intention for the future.

Whether stated or unstated, conscious or unconscious, all of us already have intentions. Although we might never speak them, we always give them power, and the type of power we give them leads to the resulting actions.

You can look at someone's actions and see what their true intentions are, just as you can observe behaviors and understand a person's true underlying passions. Actions reveal the nature and clarity of a person's intentions.

For example, a lot of people's lives have recurring themes: *I want to. I hope it will happen. I'll get to it sometime. I wish I'd done that.*

They spend time looking in the rearview mirror instead of gazing out the windshield. They have a wish or a hope, but not intention. Intention is a decision to act upon a wish or a desire and achieve it.

No matter where you are in your career or life, it's never too late to start on a journey that positively impacts an emerging leader. Excellent mentors lead by example. You can't succeed as a mentor without having clear intentions and skill in manifesting your own dreams and mission. You also need to have clear intentions about what kind of qualities you want to develop in potential mentees and how.

> *Intention to mentor others has a "why" that is grounded in the highest and greatest good of all.*

Your intention to mentor others has a "why" that is grounded in the highest and greatest good of all. It comes from deep within, excites you, and maybe even makes you a bit nervous.

But as with Sarah doing her first push-up, knowing your intentions simplifies decision making. You will know what you're all about, which will define what you give your life and time to, what matters to you, and what moves you forward in that direction.

So: take a few minutes to write down your mentoring vision/intention.

What kind of difference do you hope to make in others' lives?

_____

_____

_____

_____

How can you observe people around you to see where these things are possible?

_____

_____

_____

_____

The Power of Sociograms

There's a great technique for observing people in more depth, and I found to my surprise that I actually do it naturally. Maybe you do, too.

When I'm watching people, I have this habit of arranging and grouping things in my mind. It's how my mind naturally and subconsciously works. I'm an arranger. Do you have crazy subconscious abilities you've been blessed with? They may help you in ways you're not even aware of.

When I first realized this aspect of myself, I thought it was just a weird quirk. But as I've matured, I've realized it's actually a gift, and I've used it to my advantage.

This gift allows me to mentally create what are called "sociograms," which are diagrams illustrating people's behaviors. While most people draw the diagram, I don't have to; I can see it in my imagination.

I was introduced to the sociogram idea early in my career. It is a tool for charting the relationships within a group. A sociogram shows each person's social links and preferences, which can be very valuable data for leaders.

The thing I love about sociograms is that they show me who has influence within the group. For instance, in the sociogram example shown here (created at BeyondLuna.com), the lines with arrows illustrate one-way influence, and the thicker, non-arrow lines illustrate two-way influence. Note that no one in this example is influenced but does not have influence.

As I sit high in the bleachers, observing sporting events, my mind is putting together a sociogram of the assembled group. In these informal situations, I don't always have the luxury to learn whether my observations are correct, or whether those that have influence truly understand the power in it, or whether they see themselves in the way I see them. But it's an interesting mental exercise that helps me see more than I would otherwise.

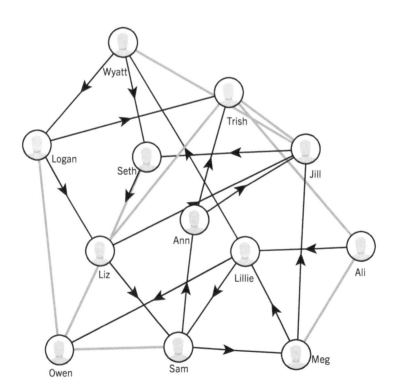

Sociograms might help you to create pictures of your observations and choose whom you will mentor. To learn how to create one, here's a great exercise.

Creating a Sociogram

1. Think of a situation where you have observed a group of people for long enough to understand their influence on each other—perhaps in your work situation, your family, at church, or in another organization. Place a character in the middle of the diagram. They need not be the most important; they're just a starting point. With a larger organization, you may not even know some people's names, but you can use other ways to describe them, such as "Jane's secretary" or "the deacon with the silver hair."
2. Position other characters around the first one, based on their relationship with that person. If possible, position them nearer each other based on the closer and better their relationships. You'll start to notice clusters of closer interactions, with others more on their "outskirts." For instance, in my example, Trish, Jill, and Wyatt are all good friends who influence each other, but they don't really know Sam at all, and while two of them know and influence Seth, he doesn't really influence them.
3. Though my example is simple, you can get as creative and detailed as you like. For instance, you can use dotted, bold, or jagged lines to show the nature of the relationships between all of the characters as being minimal, close, or tense. You could even use certain colors of lines or arrows for positive vs. negative influence—green for positive, red for negative, yellow for neutral.

4. After charting your sociogram, take a deeper look at the groups or cliques. Who talks to whom? Who doesn't talk to whom? Who has the most or least influence?

Want an easy way to create a quick sociogram? You can do it online at BeyondLuna.com.

Your Observational Superpowers

Okay, I realize not everyone goes around with sociograms in their heads like I do. But that's okay—it's just one way to observe. If creating a sociogram seems too complicated, there are plenty of other natural ways to identify potential mentees.

For instance, sometimes, a mentor homes in on a person's discomfort to try to identify and help resolve the issue.

This was the situation with one of my friends, Daniela, who is an assistant professor in linguistics.

Rather than seeing a classroom full of students, Daniela sees each student as an individual and intentionally finds ways to know them on a professional and appropriate personal level. She asks powerful questions on assignments, engages students one on one, listens for understanding, and watches behavior. It's a magical mix.

Daniela recently told me about a situation with a student she had mentored named Bailey. Daniela had observed that Bailey seemed very uncomfortable during their first class. Daniela hoped Bailey's answers to her "get to know you" assignment would give some insight into her hesitation.

Daniela's hopes proved fruitful. Bailey's answers sparked a quick follow-up conversation, revealing that she was a film production major and hoped to live abroad one day. However, she had strong apprehensions about her skills in Spanish.

With Bailey's vision of her future in mind, Daniela challenged and supported her throughout the semester, engaging with her during office hours and special sessions where students could practice their language skills. Bailey did very well in the course, and her language skills skyrocketed. She had just needed to be "seen" and have some life spoken into her to counteract her apprehension.

Daniela continued to mentor Bailey throughout her college experience, and within a year after graduating, Bailey was working full-time in the film industry and living in Spain. She had not only overcome her apprehension of a basic Spanish course, but she was also now living in a Spanish-speaking country! She had achieved her vision.

Note that Daniela didn't necessarily choose to mentor every student in the class in this manner. The same situation or approach wouldn't always apply to other students. Each situation develops in its own way.

What to Look for in a Potential Mentee

Both Daniela and I approach mentoring somewhat differently, but we also have some things in common. When looking for potential mentees, we both observe three different things about people:

- Ability—what are they capable of doing?

- Motivation—what drives them to do things, and what are they willing to do?

- Attitude—how open are they to learning and constructive criticism, and how well will they deal with setbacks?

Just as Daniela and I don't always take the same approach in observing, neither will you. Your own "observational superpowers" will develop based on your intention and the way your own unique strengths factor in the way you observe others.

If you're not sure what your strengths are, I recommend a great assessment tool called CliftonStrengths. You can take the assessment at www.gallup.com. Using that, you'll be able to quickly identify your own strengths and clarify how they might help you observe and mentor others—especially in helping you find those whose skills yours will complement as a mentor. You won't be able to help another much who already is strong in all the areas you are.

Find the True Leaders

Sociograms help show the influencers in a group. Whether they see themselves as "leaders" or are in positions of "official authority" in the group doesn't matter—and neither does their type of influence, whether positive or negative. Either way, they are your leaders.

When identifying emerging leaders, it helps to keep two things in mind: their actions and their positions.

Leaders Solve Problems and Serve People

My friend, Dr. Tim Elmore, is the CEO of Growing Leaders. He's had a lot of experience observing leadership. He describes leaders as those who "solve problems and serve people."

Not only do I love the essence of that statement, but I love the fact that it's easy to observe both of those actions. Sitting in the gym or auditorium, I can easily see those leaders. They are the ones who run to get the loose ball for the referee, offer a hand to help the fallen opponent, come forward to help the teacher with technology, set props for the next scene, and hold the door for the elderly couple as they leave the performance. In a corporate setting, these are the people who step up to help solve problems beyond their job description, reach out to mentor co-workers, help new people settle in, make an extra effort to help customers, and stand up for others who are being dealt with unfairly.

These are all examples of organically developed young leaders who are solving problems and serving people most of the time without being told to do so. They may not even think of themselves as leaders, yet they have the hearts of leaders and the courage to put leadership into action.

Position Isn't Everything

Early one school year while I was the director for personal and professional leadership development in the Krannert School of Management at Purdue University, a student leadership group invited me to replace their current advisor, who would be stepping away in a month. I was pleased to have that month to observe the workings of the group before assuming the advisor role.

I quickly noticed a young man named Chase, who sat in a fairly prominent spot but didn't say much. During several meetings, the elected leader specifically asked Chase his opinion on important topics, and this young man always had significant insight.

Leaders of disposition almost always have more influence than leaders of position.

Wanting to harness Chase's power, I encouraged him to continue to seek leadership opportunities. He did, but always in an understated, yet powerful way.

As I came to know Chase better, I realized he was a leader of "disposition" vs. a leader of "position."

A leader of **position** is someone in an official leadership role. The elected leader was a positional leader—he had an officially recognized leadership position in the group.

However, Chase was a dispositional leader. Dispositional leadership is not about the role; it's about the goal. Leaders of **disposition** do not necessarily have (or want) a position of any official authority, as do leaders of position, who are elected or appointed a title. Yet leaders of disposition almost always have more influence than leaders of position. A person's disposition is the way they communicate themselves through verbal or nonverbal cues. Again, this can be a positive or negative influence; Chase happened to be a leader with super-positive influence.

Chase was the boyfriend (and is now the husband) of the president of the student council, who was, and still is, a strong positional female leader. Chase's younger brother, another impactful leader, was past president of the Leadership Academy. Though Chase himself did not hold the highest official level of leadership in any organization, he influenced many areas of the school not just due to his connections but because of his disposition. He had a superb social-emotional understanding of himself and others, positioned himself in places where he could serve well based on his skills and abilities, and was an exceptional listener and discerner—the most skilled I have ever known of anyone his young age.

Chase was the one I had my impressionable son sit beside during social outings when I could bring my family along. He was one I purposefully tapped to help re-vamp and lead the yearly leadership conference to add more leadership development opportunities within the school. His servant leadership position was a highly visible position with students, staff, and alumni.

Had I not observed the situation with an open mind and instead looked strictly at the slate of officers of these student groups to find potential leaders, I would not have seen Chase's value. He would have had an impact anyway, but I like to think that with my observation and encouragement, Chase was able to serve in a greater capacity, positively influence more people and situations, and leave a lasting legacy in the school.

Find the influencers—they are already leading.

Take a good, clear look at the influential behaviors (both good and bad) of those in your areas of influence. Find the influencers—they are already leading. Having a clear understanding of their real potential is the first and a very important step in developing them.

Exercise: Vision and Action

To clarify your intentions and improve your observation methods for finding others to mentor, one of the easiest starting points is a quick self-assessment.

Why assess yourself before assessing others? Self-assessment gives you a framework to connect your strengths and focus areas to theirs. You can't observe others as potential mentees if you aren't clearly aware of yourself and how you might be able to help them.

I suggest you start with my "three spheres" approach. You will assess potential mentees with this model, so assessing yourself with it first is a great way to start thinking along those lines.

Start with creating a mind map of areas where you have some expertise in each sphere. To get you started thinking, take a look at the example providing some general topics in each sphere.

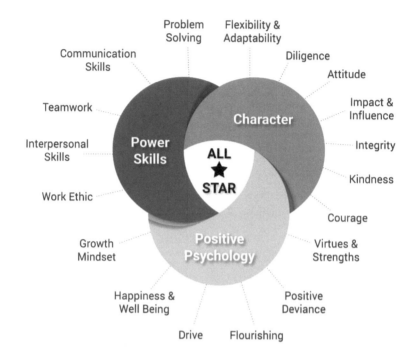

Now fill the map with areas of expertise you could use in a mentoring relationship.

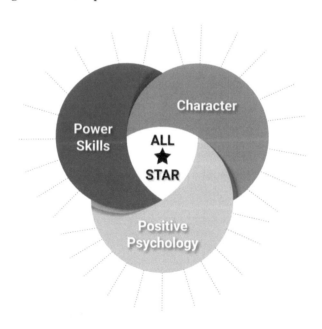

Exercise: Find Your 'Bucket List' of Chosen Leaders

Take a week to really observe people in your surroundings. Then make a list. Who are the young people in your midst who solve problems and serve others? Try to think of as many as you can.

Sample Entries

Each entry in your list should look something like this:

Name: Jane Smith
Problems solved/How: Excellent customer service, especially good at resolving complaints. Beautifully handled Mr. Jones' problem last week. Is also very good at explaining our processes to new staff.

Others served/How: Customers with complaints/resolving the issues; new staff/helping train and acclimatize them; management/helps train new staff, freeing up management time for other higher-level things only they can attend to.

Name: Nick (oldest son)
Problems solved/How: Super-organized and helpful; helped my spouse pack the car for camping when I didn't have time to; drove his younger siblings to and from school on time every day last week; brought me dinner after practice Wednesday on spouse's request, to make sure I ate something when I was working late at the office.

Others served/How: The kids, me, my spouse, and indirectly, my staff and co-workers, because his help allowed me to stay focused on and complete our big proposal on time.

Try to come up with a total of twenty people on your list.

Sorting Your Buckets

Now that you have a starting list, let's add to it and start thinking about potential. This is how you'll see undeveloped skills and qualities just waiting for the chance to manifest.

Let's start by classifying the people you've observed. To think deep and wide, use the four-bucket approach outlined below. Your final goal is to have four individuals in each bucket, for a total of sixteen people. That's fewer than your twenty above, but that's all right; as you are sorting them, you'll have more of some and less of others for each bucket, so it's good to have more to start with.

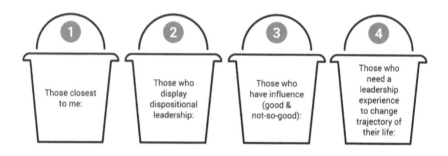

4 Buckets of Leadership Potential

1. Those closest to me:
2. Those who display dispositional leadership:
3. Those who have influence (good & not-so-good):
4. Those who need a leadership experience to change trajectory of their life:

To fill the buckets, think about this: who in your list is operating at around average performance but, with development, could become an All-Star?

Bucket 1: Those Closest to You

This bucket will probably contain your children, extended family members, those you've chosen as family, and close friends. In your previous observation exercise, were any of the twenty people from this group? If so, put their names here. If you overlooked this group for whatever reason, now is the time to add them. They are deeply embedded within your areas of influence. (Doing a sociogram of your areas of influence might help you think of other people you're overlooking as well.)

Write your Bucket 1 names here:

1. _____
2. _____
3. _____
4. _____

Bucket 2: Dispositional Leaders
These are people who solve problems and serve people. These are people like Chase, who lead by their disposition and need more development to extend their influence. They likely don't hold a prominent position and are fairly quiet. They may shy away from "Type A" leadership but have great potential in other leadership approaches.

If you don't have your full four for this category yet, you can brainstorm in several different ways to find them. One of the best ways might be to look back at the sociograms of your areas of influence. Within those, have you noticed anyone with this type of leadership potential? If you have too many people in Bucket 1, select some of those to put here.

This bucket can also include young positional leaders who display influential qualities but need a bit of work and polishing to become better.

Write your Bucket 2 names here:

1. _____
2. _____

3. _____

4. _____

Bucket 3: Influencers (Good and Bad)
Bucket 3 holds people you've noticed as having influence (good or bad) but may not be considered "leaders" by those around them. Those with positive influence may already be in one of your buckets. If not, place them here. However, I suggest you also think about and add people who have "bad" influence. Let's face it—they're influencing others, so they probably have leadership qualities and need to be considered. We don't know why they're focused on negatively influencing others. Perhaps they've never been encouraged or taught how to have a positive influence. Maybe they don't realize that they're negatively affecting the situations they're in. Your interest in them could change their life trajectories.

Write your Bucket 3 names here:

1. _____

2. _____

3. _____

4. _____

Bucket 4: Skilled, but Not Confident
This bucket is comprised of people who have good skills in some area(s) but lack confidence or initiative. They may have no idea they could be leaders. They may have never stepped up to take a leadership role. Perhaps they don't see that type of potential in themselves.

However, not every leader is presidential material. Maybe they would enjoy leading a family business or work group someday with the right encouragement and support.

For this group, development will change their life trajectory. Remember—everyone is extraordinary. But not everyone understands that about themselves. Bucket 4 people often fly under the radar or aren't readily recognizable as leaders. But when someone chooses and speaks into them, develops them, and sets them on a different course, they could go on to become foundational leaders of our communities. Wouldn't you love to see that happen?

Write your Bucket 4 names here:

1. _____
2. _____
3. _____
4. _____

What if you find someone who fits in more than one bucket? You can put one person in multiple buckets—and if so, I suggest you put those individuals high on your list for potential development.

Take a few days—or even a week—to fill your buckets. List as many people as you can in your different buckets. Make sure to look back over your personal sociogram and ensure you haven't missed anyone.

I know; sixteen people seems like a lot, right? But that's okay. Once we get to the next chapter, you'll start narrowing the list down.

CHAPTER 2

Acknowledge

"When you see something beautiful in someone, speak it."
—RUTHIE LINDSEY

What It Means to Be Chosen

When I was ten years old, I used to shoot baskets in our family's driveway. One day, my dad came home and mentioned that one of the junior-senior high school coaches, Coach Bauer, had seen me shooting baskets in my driveway and had told him to tell me to keep shooting.

Surprised at being noticed, I did just that. Her simple encouragement to me, through my dad, inspired me to keep working on my skills—partly because I enjoyed it, but mostly because I hoped she would drive by our home again and see me shooting baskets. I wanted her to know I was listening.

Coach Bauer's Crystal Ball ability allowed her to see and develop skills to their highest potential. I don't know whether she started her career with such sharp insight into others' potential, but I can guess that she got better at it the more she practiced.

That moment when she noticed and acknowledged me definitely affected me through the following years—in fact, I know it changed my life.

For one thing, all that practice shooting baskets paid off. When I attended junior high, I became part of Coach Bauer's basketball team.

To picture what I looked like in junior high, all you need to know is that my dad's nickname for me during that time was "Olive Oyl," after the character from *Popeye*. I was tall, skinny, and only mildly coordinated, but I was eager to learn and loved playing on a team. I tried to learn everything I could as I continued to practice my skills. During that time, Coach Bauer taught us how to set goals and work toward achieving them, and I practiced doing that as well.

In addition to basketball, I also played volleyball. When I moved on to high school, I was fortunate to have Coach Bauer as my high school varsity volleyball coach. In high school, my stature and strength didn't change much, but the level of competition and intensity in sports did.

As a freshman in high school, I set my goal to play Division 1 college volleyball. I'm sure many thought I was crazy—I didn't have the physical stature, coordination, or strength to achieve it. But Coach Bauer had already noticed and chosen me because she believed in me. Her Crystal Ball told her where I could be in two days, two weeks, and two years with development of my power skills, character, and positive psychology—my three spheres.

As a freshman volleyball player, I rarely saw the playing floor, but I was blessed to play a majority of the time on the junior varsity team as a sophomore. Moving onto the varsity team my junior year was a crucible moment for me. My desire to play in college had not gone away, but my ability had not kept pace. I played just the front row, which meant I only played one-half of the available time; this was not a qualification that would get the attention of many college coaches. I needed to develop my skills in the back row to achieve the caliber needed for a Division 1 college player.

Luckily, at that point in the late 1980s, club volleyball emerged. I lived about an hour away from a volleyball "hotbed" and a very high-caliber volleyball club. My parents sacrificed in many ways to allow me the opportunity to play club volleyball. My mom drove me an hour each way to practice twice a week. My dad willingly paid the bill, and my whole family sacrificed valuable weekend and church time to spend with me at tournaments. I barely made the B (development) team and was very intimidated by the high-caliber players I played with, most of whom knew each other. I was the outsider coming from more than an hour away, and they didn't even recognize the name of my school.

Though intimidated, I observed, listened, and learned. And even though I failed often, I persisted. I knew my real work was to become a better back-row player and passer, so I studied the good players, did my best to imitate them, listened to my coaches, and put in the work. And although it was uncomfortable and hard, I kind of enjoyed being exposed to my craft at a level of excellence beyond my own abilities.

Those were all traits I had learned from Coach Bauer.

After one year of club ball, I was able to help lead my school team to the semi-state my senior year. And my "unknown" school played against the well-known teams of my club teammates. But still, no college volleyball offer came.

I persisted anyway, playing club ball during the spring of my senior year. At the last minute, my D1 college offer arrived! In those days, there were no big signing ceremonies or parties, but I didn't need a lot of people there making a fuss over me; I just needed to know in my heart that I had overcome my challenges and that my hard work had paid off. I still remember signing my National Letter of Intent in the principal's office—and since the principal happened to be my dad, I signed it on his desk. He had called my mom, and she was there, too. A local sports photographer snapped the photos as I signed my name. It's such a sweet, intimate memory. I had worked so hard to get there—and the people who supported me most were in the room with me.

None of this would have been possible without Coach Bauer, whose Crystal Ball caused her to see potential in a mildly coordinated "Olive Oyl" ten years earlier. She not only saw it; she spoke it into me, developed my functional skill, positive psychology, and character, and embedded in me the transferable leadership skills that I still use to this day.

The key to my success was that someone had not only seen my potential—they had acknowledged it. Without that crucial step, I would never have had these incredible experiences.

Speaking into Emerging Leaders

You've already developed a set of criteria to look for in your potential mentees and have clarified your goals and intent, so you are more situationally aware of opportunities for finding them. The next step is to let them know you see them. This can be a little more difficult for some mentors, especially newer ones who have less experience.

Acknowledging someone is a simple enough action in theory—you approach the person and praise them for something you've seen in their actions or behavior that illustrates good leadership.

However, verbally acknowledging someone can be intimidating. You might worry about what you should say or how you can convey sincerity. You may worry about how the person will interpret your gesture.

There are so many reasons why we might shy away from verbally acknowledging someone. But think about this—it's not about what you say; it's about how you make the other person feel. Our emerging leaders are dying for sincere feedback from someone who has their best interests in mind. Young leaders need to have life spoken into them! They need to feel chosen by someone who recognizes that they are extraordinary. That someone is you!

So let me help you with a model that I discovered years ago. The "STAR Method" is actually a technique used in job interviews to gather all the relevant information about a candidate's specific capabilities based on the position requirements. However, it also works very well for acknowledging and "speaking life" into emerging leaders. By identifying something specific you've observed in them, you make it more than a hollow compliment. And as a bonus, the system is easy to remember.

The STAR Method

The STAR method is useful in the moment, when you observe something you want to acknowledge.

STAR stands for Situation, Task, Action, and Result:

- **Situation:** In what situation did the person demonstrate leadership?
- **Task:** What task(s) was the emerging leader carrying out?
- **Action:** What leadership actions did the leader take?
- **Result:** What positive results did those actions achieve?

Speaking into Emerging Leaders with STAR:

Situation:
In what situation did the emerging leader demonstrate leadership?

Example: At our recent guest speaker's presentation

Task:
What specific task(s) was the emerging leader carrying out?

Example: You came forward and helped with the technology issue

Action:
What leadership action(s) did the emerging leader take?

Example: You took initiative where you could help

Result:
What result(s) did the emerging leader's actions achieve?

Example: You put the speaker at ease and solved the technology issue

As a mentor, it's important to keep this STAR method top of mind and use it multiple times a day. The more you follow this method, the easier it becomes until (hopefully) it becomes a habit. The results may surprise you. It's vital to acknowledge and speak life into those we are mentoring. They need positive feedback for inspiration and motivation. They need to feel appreciated. Let's face it: we all need these things.

After you have praised the observed qualities, you can ask, "What other areas of leadership would you like to develop or improve?" And LISTEN. Their answer will make your next step as their mentor easier.

Exercise: Acknowledge One of Your Chosen

Take a look at your "bucket" exercise and what you wrote about the people who solved problems and served others. Thinking about the situation, take a few moments and work through the STAR Method for that person, describing each element.

Person: _____

Situation: _____

Task: _____

Action: _____

Result: _____

Wasn't that easy? All right—now you're ready to approach the person and give them the above information. That's right; tell them! Don't they deserve to know that you are impressed with what they did? If someone noticed something good about you, wouldn't you want to know?

If you're not quite ready to voice your observations to people, try keeping a journal for a while with some notes on your observations. Use the STAR format to record what you see. After you've become more comfortable observing this way, you'll start getting more confident in approaching people with your observations.

Sometimes, these small observations are the only encounters you may have with people. You won't become their full-fledged, official mentor. But you can still make a difference in their lives by noticing and praising what they are doing.

Meanwhile, if you're trying to determine where to forge a true mentoring relationship, the next step is looking at whether and how you might be able to help.

CHAPTER 3

Evaluate

"The quality of a leader is reflected in the standards they set for themselves."

—RAY KROC

Behaviors Point to Passion

When you're looking at someone and trying to decide how to acknowledge them, it's good to also note other things about them. Some people are skilled, but they don't have the passion to fuel their potential. How do you recognize when to work with someone and when you might be trying to develop someone who isn't interested?

The first key is to evaluate their behaviors in relation to their goals. As I've mentioned previously, more often than not, behaviors point to passion. If they're passionate about their goals, you'll know by their behavior.

Here's an example. I'll never forget my first year of teaching and coaching. I had chosen to coach the seventh-grade girls' basketball team. Our team was shaping up nicely in the preseason, and I was excited when the day of our first game came. I must admit, I was pretty confident heading into the game. Our warm-up was looking really good, and the other team wasn't looking all that strong. I was hoping for a strong first win.

With about two minutes left of warm-ups, the tallest and one of the most talented girls on my team skipped over to me at the bench. In all seriousness she asked, "Are we going to be able to go to the locker room and freshen up before the game?" I couldn't believe what my ears were hearing, and I tried not to show my true emotions. I kindly said, "No, there won't be time," and ushered her back onto the court. And for the remaining two minutes of warm-ups, my confidence waned.

I don't remember the outcome of the game, but I have told that story nearly a hundred times in the past twenty-eight years due to the lesson it taught me. Though this young lady was one of the most talented players on the team, her actions told me she was not the most passionate about basketball. It wouldn't be a waste of time to help develop her, but if I needed to make decisions about how to prioritize my time with whom, this was one of the main signals I used. It showed me to prioritize others first who may have had less initial talent but more drive to achieve the goals.

Passion Overcomes Pain

One main reason to look at passion is because it's an internal quality that will help a person overcome all obstacles—including the different kinds of "pain" they will suffer as they work to succeed and encounter setbacks. It's part of a person's positive psychology—one of the three spheres of leadership.

Passion drives behavior through difficulties. In fourth grade, I had a really cool teacher who loved her calling, had a sense of humor, and best of all, read chapter books to us after coming in from noontime recess and gave us full-size candy bars when we finished learning our multiplication tables. She also happened to be the wife of our high school athletic director. Since my dad was the high school principal, she and I could relate to each other's daily lives very well.

Just after Thanksgiving, my class was out on the playground for recess, and our usual group that played either kickball or dodgeball had chosen dodgeball that day. Our usual playing field was a little soggy after a rain, so we were playing on the blacktop basketball court. While attempting to make an amazing jumping dodge, I came down hard on the blacktop. Although I didn't hit my head, it was one of those types of falls where you see stars for a few moments afterward.

I quickly brushed off the pain because I was one of the last players still in the game. Recess quickly came to an end. I went for a drink of water and settled in at my desk, ready to listen to my teacher read the next chapter of *James and the Giant Peach* to the class. I don't remember much about it because I was trying to ignore the huge sense of pain radiating from my left arm, which had taken the brunt of my fall.

I managed through the rest of the afternoon and boarded the school bus. During my ride home, my arm still really hurt, but I knew that if I told my parents how badly it hurt that I'd have to go to the doctor and potentially miss the varsity basketball game on Friday night. This was Wednesday afternoon. So, I toughed it out for the next few days.

My teacher had been observing me for those few days. While sitting next to my mom at the home basketball game that Friday night, my teacher clued my mom in on the pain I was experiencing (and not claiming). So, on Saturday morning, my parents came and woke me up to find out how badly my arm hurt. I answered, "a lot," and immediately broke into tears.

A quick trip to the ER revealed that my arm was indeed broken. My parents felt awful that I had endured this pain, and they hadn't noticed. I quickly confessed I hid it from them because I was afraid I would have missed the game. You see, I love to watch ball games and eat popcorn, and that passion was evident to me even in early elementary school. My behavior (and endurance of pain) pointed to my passion.

Passion fuels dedication. Would someone without a passion for what they're doing work through a painful situation to keep doing it? Would they have the discipline to practice every day?

As a mentor, are you paying attention to the behaviors of those you are developing? Can you readily see their passions from their behaviors? What natural passions do you see in those you are developing?

Think about the leaders you've placed in your buckets. What have you observed of their passions? What pain are they willing to overcome or ignore because of them? Take some quick notes on what you've seen or are presently observing. These will help you later when you start narrowing down your priority people to focus on.

Observational Assessment: The Three Spheres of Leadership

To be successful at an All-Star level, leaders must have the highest caliber power skills, character, and positive psychology—the three spheres we looked at earlier when you did your own self-assessment.

Think about the high-caliber leaders you have known. How did they demonstrate excellence in these three areas? What kinds of power skills (also known as soft skills—though I believe there is nothing "soft" about them) did they possess? How did they show their strength of character? How did the strength and flexibility within their psyche factor into their suc-

> *To be successful at an All-Star level, leaders must have the highest caliber power skills, character, and positive psychology.*

cess? How did these three work together to overcome obstacles and achieve goals?

Now, just for effect, let's look at them in reverse:

- How many high-caliber leaders do you know that lack **power skills**? Lack of power skills does not make an All-Star.

- How many high-caliber leaders lack **character**? Lack of character does not make an All-Star.

- How many high-caliber leaders whom you know lack **positive mindset** (psychology)? Negative mindset does not make an All-Star.

Let's face it; we all need continual work in all three of these areas, no matter how well we've developed ourselves. However, All-Star leaders perform strongly in all three of these areas without lack.

If your mentee is lacking in any of the above areas, it will affect everything else. But probably most important of all of them is their positive psychology—their true knowledge of their authentic self. Their psyche is where their passions form—and as the stories at the beginning of the chapter show, passions drive interest and values, which then drive focus and success. Without passion, it's tough to stay motivated or focused on improvement and development.

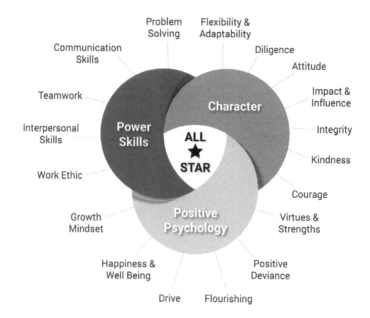

A person can't change their passions—they either have a passion for something, or they don't. Since passion fuels the drive to do everything else, your mentee needs to truly know and respect his or her authentic self before embarking on new skill-building activities. If they're building their skills in an area they aren't passionate about or that doesn't support their passions, they won't feel fulfilled or motivated after a while. Probably one of the most important things you as a mentor can do is to know your mentee's real passion and keep it in mind even when they try to talk themselves out of it. And believe me, they do!

Next comes character—because that involves integrity and attitude. If they don't have a positive attitude, they won't be open to learning the necessary skills, and without integrity, they won't have a solid focus on exceptional quality nor take responsibility for their own development. As a mentor, you can help them build and reinforce their own positive attitude and be an accountability partner for them.

And then, of course, there are power skills. These are skills such as interpersonal communication and teamwork skills. Some skills will already be present through talents developed naturally—but others might be unknown areas where they've never been trained and don't necessarily know how to proceed, even in looking for and evaluating the best learning opportunities. That's where you can help them, too.

If you've already been mentoring people, you probably already know how to evaluate the three spheres of leadership, at least somewhat, in your own way. Even if you've never mentored anyone and you've mostly been focused on developing these qualities in yourself, you'll still learn to quickly recognize where your mentees are getting off track in the above areas. (Keep that in mind, as we'll go into it more later in the chapter.)

In addition to the preceding three spheres assessment, which I feel is a foundational observation to work from, you can use many other tools and perspectives to assess people's qualities and get a sense of what they might need from you. Let's take a look at a few others.

Take a Strengths Inventory

"I feel robbed!" Those were my sentiments after attending my first strengths workshop. Why was I fifteen years into my career and just now introduced to this life-changing material? What I had discovered about myself would have helped me fast-track my career!

Though I had had a blessed career up to that point, I couldn't help but wonder how knowing my strengths would have changed it. I would have done my work differently. Based on my strengths, I would have chosen different roles to impact the organizations in which I worked. I would have chosen different projects in which my strengths could make a deeper impact. With a clearer idea of who I was, I would have lived more fully and confidently as a young professional.

Letting my anger and disappointment spur me into action, I vowed right then and there to be the change I wanted to see. I became a student of the CliftonStrengths assessment and spent the time and money to become a Gallup-Certified Strengths Coach. It's a title and tool I intend to use for the rest of my life.

Insight into a person's strengths is crucial when mentoring them. You can rely on your own observation, but it's not as accurate as having them do an assessment. In my conversations, so many of my mentees have gone on to tell me how vital their strengths assessment was in helping them make decisions and plan their careers. Advising them to do this early can help them eliminate a lot of unnecessary and deflating challenges before they even face them.

For instance, the CliftonStrengths assessment measures your talents—your natural patterns of thinking, feeling, and behaving—and categorizes them into the thirty-four CliftonStrengths themes. Your customized report reveals your top five themes that help you chart your course to accomplish great things using what you naturally do best. And when you consider how all of one's top strengths work together, it can lead to fascinating insights.

Your mentee can benefit by using his or her strengths to determine the best career options and training opportunities, decide on job roles that would work best for them, and determine how to work with others to ensure their strengths complement each other's and achieve the best results.

Plug the Holes

Recently, a football coach attended one of my strengths workshops. During a break, we were debating the concept of solely focusing on strengths. He looked directly at me and said, "Sharlee, my job as a coach is to accentuate the strengths of my team, but I also have to plug the holes of our weaknesses. My offense is kind of like a boat. I can win if I accentuate my player's talents and strengths, but I will certainly lose if I don't plug the holes (quite literally on my offense line)." I gained a refined perspective on developing leaders that day, and that is why this step of assessment is so pertinent to the process.

No matter how many great people you have on a team, if someone isn't performing in a certain area, it can affect everything. Think of an assembly line. If someone in a position in the middle doesn't know how to do their job properly, it affects the rest of the people down the line. Each person who doesn't know how to do their job affects the quality of the item, building mistake upon mistake and creating delays and other issues. Even if everyone does well except the person at the end, that one person will still create a flawed product. If management doesn't identify and plug these quality "holes," the entire team's performance will suffer.

In assembly lines, it's easy to see the effects of not plugging these holes, but in everyday life, it can be more difficult to notice or even to own where one's own efforts (or lack of them) are taking a toll. As a result, it often looks like "other people's fault."

That's why emerging leaders need mentors. Mentors help them see what's going on from another perspective and look into their blind spots. For instance, I recall one young leader who I'll call Jake, who had just started an entry-level position after graduating from college. He was a true people person and always focused on getting along well with everyone, which worked fine during college for the most part. However, moving into a work situation brought new challenges.

Jake was also very quality-conscious, and he quickly noticed some of his teammates in his new work environment didn't seem to be as careful. Because he was evaluated on his team's entire performance, their issues were also hampering his standing with his supervisor.

Because he didn't like to deal with conflict, he didn't know how to address the concerns he had. He didn't want to say anything to his teammates for fear of alienating them, especially since he was the "new kid on the block" and still learning the ropes himself.

Jake would go home frustrated every night, complaining to friends and family about the poor work environment. However, one of his mentors finally asked him an important question. "How have you tried to address it?"

Of course, Jake hadn't tried confronting anyone. He felt trapped and resigned to just being an unhappy observer.

But his mentor challenged him to try a different approach. Instead of blaming them and going home frustrated every night, he did some thinking and research on ways to approach some of the situations differently. He also did some role-playing with his mentor to figure out the best approaches he would be comfortable with. Armed with this information, Jake started respectfully requesting what he needed from his co-workers so he could complete his own work to his quality standards, explaining why, so they would realize he wasn't pointing fingers but trying to make the end product as good as possible.

Though there were some misunderstandings sometimes, Jake learned to weather those and stay true to his cause, which was to benefit his entire team through improving their work. As a result, misunderstandings had little long-term effect, and best of all, the team eventually became much stronger and was able to identify some process and time constraint issues that had been creating some of the difficulties. They brought suggestions to their supervisor for rectifying these, further enabling their performance to improve.

By owning that he had a hole to plug in his own skills, and by taking the time to learn how to do that, Jake took responsibility for himself and his team's quality instead of being constantly disappointed and frustrated with his teammates. As a result, his supervisor and his team saw him as someone who could solve problems and serve people instead of someone who just complained about them.

To assess means to evaluate or estimate the nature, ability, or quality of.[14] Assessment comes in many forms. We assess qualities through tools and methods such as tests or quizzes, written observations, verbal feedback, or even something as simple as watching game film to see what the team did or didn't do well.

Assessments can be highly detailed or simple. The key is to use a measuring stick so those being assessed know how they measure up, what they are doing right, and what holes they need to plug. To put it simply, it's like getting a test back and going over it so you know what you did right and what you still need to work on and learn.

---

14 *Oxford English Dictionary*, s.v. "assess (v.)," https://www.google.com/search?client=firefox-b-1-d&q=definition+assess.

Useful Assessment Tools

If you really like the idea of using assessment tools and want to go beyond the CliftonStrengths, I wholeheartedly support you. The more information you and your Chosen have, the easier it will be for you to work together. And proven assessment tools are likely to be far more accurate than just relying on your own interpretation, as personal perceptions often get clouded (either positively or negatively) by assumptions and projections we're unaware of.

I've provided a list below of some helpful tools, but don't let that overwhelm you. You don't have to do all of them. They're just there for suggestions, especially if you need something specific and aren't sure where to find it.

If you have no idea where to start, I suggest starting with CliftonStrengths. If you don't want to get too in-depth but you want something in addition to CliftonStrengths, I'd suggest having your Chosen also take a personality assessment if he/she hasn't done so already. I believe strength discovery and personality type is the trailhead to a journey of growth and development. These two assessments will really clarify their general approach to problem-solving, communication, and various other things. The rest delve more deeply into specific areas of development.

Note that many assessments have free versions that offer a "lite" version of the assessment. If you want to suggest a tool to your Chosen, try taking the assessment first to test its usefulness. (You may learn something new about yourself, too!) Then you'll know if the "lite" version gets to the level of learning you want. If not, it might be worth paying for the full assessment.

Understanding Authentic Self

Myers Briggs Type Indicator (MBTI)

- Helps identify one's unique personality.
- Helps one achieve greater self-awareness.
- Provides knowledge to improve interpersonal relationships and personal wellbeing.
- Paid version: https://www.mbtionline.com/en-US/Products/For-you
- Free version: https://my-personality-test.com

YouScience

- Offers a career assessment, which is great for students or those seeking to change careers.
- Shows how one is wired and what motivates one.
- Uncovers unique skills and talents that can be used in position oneself.
- Helps one choose the best career path.
- Paid version: https://resources.youscience.com/buy

DiSC

- A different type of personality and **behavioral** assessment that divides people into four main groups of Dominance, Influence, Steadiness, and Conscientiousness.
- Helps understand and improve interpersonal communications.
- Helps connect with others more effectively.
- Helps understand how to better achieve success.
- Paid version: https://www.discprofile.com
- Free version: https://discpersonalitytesting.com/free-disc-test

Assessments for Positive Psychology

Wellbeing: The Five Essential Elements (book)

- Explains the contributors to your wellbeing over a lifetime.
- Includes a code to take the Wellbeing Finder assessment, which measures you in the five essential elements of wellbeing: Career Wellbeing, Social Wellbeing, Financial Wellbeing, Physical Wellbeing, and Community Wellbeing.
- Order the book at the Gallup Store: https://store.gallup.com/p/en-us/10410/wellbeing:-the-five-essential-elements

Reiss Motivation Assessment

- Can help a mentee who's feeling uninspired.
- Can help improve your mentoring skills.
- Identifies primary areas of motivation.
- Helps avoid being tempted into unproductive behaviors.
- Helps find and create the best, most productive environments where a person will naturally be happier.
- Paid version: https://www.reissmotivationprofile.com/products

Character Development

Habitudes is the greatest character development curriculum I've discovered in my career. It's why I became a Certified Advisor with Growing Leaders. If you want to know more about this curriculum that teaches leadership habits and attitudes, contact me.

Habitudes website: www.growingleaders.com

Assessments for Power Skills

CliftonStrengths Talent Assessment
- Discover your natural talents and develop them into strengths.
- Use your reports to maximize your potential in careers, relationships, and more.
- Paid version: https://www.gallup.com/cliftonstrengths

Fascinate
- A personal branding assessment based on a person's current marketing info.
- Helps one know how they can be seen at their best.
- Identifies what they're already doing right so they can keep doing it.
- Shows how they are most likely to influence others.
- Helps make better first impressions by learning precise words to describe themselves in interpersonal introductions, professional bios, or LinkedIn summaries.
- Since I am a Fascinate Certified Advisor, I can get discounted assessments. Contact me for pricing! To learn more, visit https://www.howtofascinate.com

Working Genius
- A strengths-based tool that classifies people within six types of "working genius": Wonder, Invention, Discernment, Galvanize, Enablement, and Tenacity (WIDGET).
- Helps one find the right kind of work/job roles.
- Helps enable more satisfying and productive relationships with family and others.

- Helps avoid demotivating situations that drain enthusiasm.
- Paid version: https://www.workinggenius.com

Exercise: The Three Spheres Assessment

Take a look at your short list of emerging leaders. Once you have acknowledged them, how do you determine where to start with development? I'm guessing you already have some ideas, but a tailored, specific assessment will help you identify the strengths and the holes you need to plug.

Part 1: The Assessment

To start, let's assess which of the three spheres is strongest and which is the weakest. Look into your own Crystal Ball to fill out the following graphic for each of your mentees, focusing on both strengths and weaknesses in each sphere. Be sure to note which are strengths and which are areas for improvement. (The graphic is here for inspiration, but you can also write these on your own piece of paper, listing each of the spheres as a header and then putting the qualities under each. If you want to use the graphic for each person, you can go to my website at SharleeLyons.com/toolkit and download a PDF mentoring toolkit, from which you can print as many copies of this graphic as you need.)

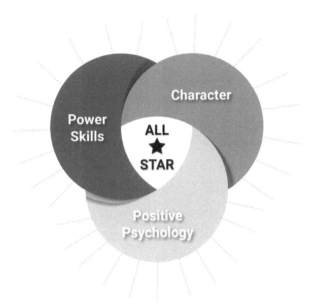

Now, examine your assessment and ask yourself the following questions for each person.

- Which sphere has the potential of sinking this emerging leader's boat unless we plug the holes?
- In which sphere does this emerging leader have the most capability right now?
- Which sphere falls in the middle of the other two—a few holes to plug, balanced by some good strengths?

Part 2: Take the Best Approach

In my experience, the best approach is one that not only builds the leader's confidence through some quick wins but also creates enough challenge that they feel they've accomplished something to be proud of.

Therefore, I recommend starting in the "middle sphere" rather than the strongest or weakest areas.

Mentors often think they should start with the largest area of deficit—in other words, the sphere that has the potential of sinking the emerging leader's ship. The mentor wants to save them or change them right now. After all, this is the biggest problem and the place where they'll see the greatest improvement, right?

However, consider the young person's psyche. They may not be emotionally or physically ready to tackle a huge deficit. It may be too overwhelming and difficult. As a result, they may suddenly balk at the idea of development, which they once thought would be so awesome. (And they may come away disliking you.) You don't want to lose them for good.

I also don't recommend starting with the sphere where the emerging leader has the most capability for two reasons:

1. Less challenge means less improvement, which could diminish their sense of accomplishment.

2. Quite frankly, they'll get a false sense of security that this development process is going to be easy, which will lead to disappointment later.

In their middle sphere, the leaders see they have some skill but know they have room for improvement, and the improvement feels challenging but not overwhelming to tackle. Working in this sphere allows them to gain momentum with their success. It's a more balanced approach, especially for someone less confident who needs to see leaps of success early in the process to motivate them to pursue more development and gain momentum.

So, which area is your Chosen's strongest? Which is weakest? Now you know the middle by default. Once you've identified it, start thinking about some ways to develop it. As you move into the next section, you'll get plenty of great tips on what to do next.

"Good leaders develop ideas. Great leaders develop people. The best leaders develop new leaders."

—BOBBY UMAR

STEP 2

DEVELOP

CHAPTER 4

Expect

"High achievement always takes place in the
framework of high expectation."

—CHARLES KETTERING

Your expectations shape the entire relationship with your mentees. If you expect nothing but All-Star performance from your Chosen, they will sense your confidence in them and perform at a higher level.

The results of an interesting Harvard University experiment illustrate this beautifully, as told by Alix Spiegel of NPR.[15]

In 1964, Prof. Howard Rosenthal conducted an experiment in a California elementary school in which he packaged a standard IQ test as a different kind of test designed to find students whose

---

15 A. Spiegel, (2012) Teachers' Expectations Can Influence How Students Perform, NPR, September 17, https://www.npr.org/sections/health-shots/2012/09/18/161159263/teachers-expectations-can-influence-how-students-perform

IQs were about to take off and bloom with the right attention. The teachers knew nothing about the true nature of the experiment.

The researchers had the teachers give the test to all students. Afterward, the researchers selected students randomly from different classes, designating them as "special."

"As he followed the children over the next two years, Rosenthal discovered that the teachers' expectations of these kids really did affect the students," Spiegel wrote.

"If teachers had been led to expect greater gains in IQ, then increasingly, those kids gained more IQ," Rosenthal noted.

"As Rosenthal did more research, he found that expectations affect teachers' moment-to-moment interactions with the children they teach in a thousand almost invisible ways," Spiegel wrote. "Teachers give the students that they expect to succeed more time to answer questions, more specific feedback, and more approval: they consistently touch, nod, and smile at those kids more."

These small cues make a huge difference over time.

Just think about it. When you limit your expectations, you unconsciously limit the potential of your Chosen. Negative expectations—conscious or not—could be leading you to negatively influence people without your realizing it. This is why we mentor—and why we have high expectations of our mentees. Our expectations change our entire focus as we listen to and work with them.

Stop Giving Advice

Let me take a quick moment to give you some advice: **stop giving advice.**

I know, you're probably raising your eyebrow at the irony, but hear me out.

Advice doesn't work in most cases. Especially when it's unsolicited.

This may sound counter-intuitive, but the best mentoring relationships aren't about giving advice. They're about developing a relationship, setting expectations, building confidence, and walking alongside others while they discover, develop, and deploy their own leadership ability.

Virtually no one wants to be told what to do. You change the world by your example, not by your opinion.

Your Chosen are already potential leaders. Why tell them what to do? They need to learn to figure things out for themselves. Instead of giving advice, let them help set their own expectations as you walk with them, guiding them to choose well, offering ideas and suggestions, asking the right questions to get them thinking differently—and of course, always expecting them to succeed.

Instead of needing your advice, they need you to be there, believing in them, giving them the small cues during each interaction that show them you care, you know they will succeed, and that they are Chosen to be extraordinary. And they need you to set the example they can gauge themselves by, giving everything you say credibility.

As mentors, that's what we're called to do. It's what this book is all about. It's about you yourself doing what it takes to be above average, fulfilling your calling as a mentor to grow and develop others—by helping them figure out how to develop themselves, and by putting them in situations to do so.

Developing through Expectations

When I worked at Krannert School of Management, the annual student leadership conference had run for twenty years under its original format and had become stale. In addition, its leadership board structure was no longer effective.

The dean had asked me to upgrade and reinvigorate the conference. For the past twenty years, the student leadership team had been led by co-chairs who were a part of the school's student council, and it was believed that these were the "best" students in the school.

However, I proposed the bold move of making the conference a student organization all its own, not under the umbrella of any other. This made sense, as the conference was a beast to plan and execute, demanding year-round attention to make it run properly. It needed its own group of student organizers not devoted to serving any other organizational needs.

I also had a plan for finding the first group of leaders. Over the past two years, after carefully observing every student organization and most of the students in the school, I knew their strengths and potential. I had my eye on six students with particular leadership skills and with whom I had a great relationship.

Now I just had to get them to accept the offer to do a lot more work than they were already doing—easy, right? But I had a plan for that, too.

People Buy into What They Help Create

I sent an invitation to my Chosen, inviting them to lunch during exam week. What student doesn't love a free lunch, especially during a really busy time? In return, I asked for an hour of their time. I ordered what I knew to be a favorite of their lunches (I'm not above bribery) and held the event in the most prestigious conference room at the school. I wanted them to feel special because they were.

I felt kind of like I was preparing for an episode of Shark Tank. During exam week, they'd be busy and distracted, not to mention tired. And here I was, asking them to do more. But hopefully, they'd realize it would be worth it.

As the students started arriving for the meeting, I could tell they were looking forward to our discussion (and the food!), but also that here was a set of very weary emerging leaders who were three days into exam week and ready to go home for break and sleep for about three days. My heart sank for them. I was about to make one of the biggest pitches of my life—not for myself, but for them. Could I bring them along despite the state they were in?

We started with lunch. Good food is good for the soul. And I provided great caffeinated drinks. They perked up a bit. After about twenty minutes of conversation, connection, and caring, I shifted gears and started my presentation. I started with the history of the conference's mission and beginnings, then laid out the present state of the conference.

Looking around the room, I could tell we'd hit a low point. I had to muster everything in me to pick this thing back up. I paused, took a deep breath, and then painted a picture of what future conferences might look like and how they could benefit our students. I ended by asking them to help create and implement a new generation of Doster Leadership Conferences.

And a funny thing happened. Because now, each one of them had a sparkle in their eye, and they started asking questions. What did I think would work? Who would help? What did the students want out of an improved conference? I had some ideas, but I purposefully didn't give those. Instead, I answered their questions with questions, getting them to think about it more themselves.

The possibilities and excitement started filling the room. As the conversation came to a crescendo, I pulled out dessert to sweeten the deal.

I could guarantee them nothing except that I would be right beside them the entire way and that we'd have some fun in the midst of the hard work. I reminded them, "Together we can do hard things." And with that, I asked them to continue to think about the possibilities and determine whether they would be on the team. I requested an answer by Christmas Eve—two weeks away.

> **Together we can do hard things.**

They left the room with leftover food and a pep in their step (thank goodness for caffeine). Now alone, before starting to clean up, I just sat down. I felt like a lawyer who had made her case, and now the decision was in the jury's hands.

The week finished, students left campus for home, and the holiday break started. I spent the next week finishing my Christmas shopping, getting groceries, making plans for holiday meals, cleaning the house for guests, and putting the finishing touches on my holiday décor. Taking a break from the holiday hustle, I checked my email and saw messages from two of the prospective conference leaders. Nervously, I decided there was no better time to "rip the band-aid off." Both of them had written some really nice things, but all I could do was scan the text for the word, "Yes." After finding it in both emails, I had to go back and make sure. Then I did a happy dance—two of the six were in!

Thankful I wasn't in the office sitting and waiting at my desk, I kept busy the next few days. Another "yes" came in on December 21, and another followed on December 22. I was amazed. Four of the six had agreed to do this monumental task, and they were actually looking forward to it!

On December 23, I waited until late in the day to check my email. There, the final two answers were waiting for me—both "yes."

I'm normally not the emotional type, but I backed up to my chair and sat down. A huge sense of relief welled up inside me, and I began to cry. Soon, gratitude overtook the relief. I felt so blessed to work with such selfless and excellent emerging leaders. I said a prayer of thanksgiving for each of them. I had just been given the best gift I could have received that year.

The New Year came, and with it, the semester started. Our committee had to hit the ground running. We had many major decisions to make, connections to restore and create, money to raise, and a renewed vision to communicate. We only had fifteen weeks to hit our major targets by the end of the school year, which would leave us in decent shape heading into summer. The conference would be one short month after the start of the next school year.

The student leadership committee had to work within a few non-negotiable parameters, but for the most part, the major decisions were up to them. They created a new "dream big" vision for the conference, developed a budget, and then revised their vision and budget based on reality, with a bit of a stretch attached to it.

They designed a new executive board structure, hand-picked and recruited junior co-chairs whom they would train to take their spots the following year, and built relationships and trust with the alumni advisors. They tackled logistics, negotiated contracts, and let no detail fall. They re-branded and communicated a new and exciting conference to every single student in the school. They had each other's backs when their teammates had a hard week or stumbled. They built trust, camaraderie, and lifelong friendships.

In late September, the new and improved Doster Leadership Conference, held on a corporate sponsor's campus, boasted a record attendance of both students and corporate representatives. The team had raised more funds than they had intended and were able to leave a starting budget to the following year's team. And the student feedback was through the roof. The student team had pulled off an amazing conference.

After the conferees were on the bus headed back to campus, we collapsed into our chairs and laughed at our inside jokes, made mental notes for next year, and celebrated the highlights. The student board left, and I tidied the room as I always do. Then I walked to my car and, once again, cried tears of gratitude.

Here's the thing: I could have prescribed a new and updated conference, reserved a host location, told the students whom to approach for funding, given them a marketing plan, and held organizational meetings. But we would have had the same problems we started with. The numbers would have sagged, the student leaders would have missed out on a huge development opportunity, and the conference would have been lackluster. Instead, by giving the students a few parameters and a lot of freedom, along with a huge challenge and unwavering support, we struck gold! Everyone won.

The corporate attendees couldn't wait to donate funds for next year and return as team leaders. The student board proposed the idea of their serving again as mentors to next year's newly elected board. The most telling data were the application numbers for the next year's conference—which went through the roof.

In addition, that particular student leadership team has gone on to further affirm my assessment of their potential, taking incredible positions:

- An auditor in a global public accounting firm.
- A corporate analyst in one of the oldest financial institutions in the US, which historically helped finance the construction of the Brooklyn Bridge and which currently ranks in the top five of the world's most attractive business student employers.
- A financial analyst for a major American airline.
- A consultant who provides an analytical perspective for solving problems in the consulting industry.

I have no doubt that All-Star team took what they learned and used it to start strong and go further faster in their own lives and careers.

The concept is really simple: people buy into what they help create—and especially when part of what they help create is the expectations. Creation breeds ownership. Carrying it out is the hard part—but the learning experience is worth it.

The Call to Leadership

I had targeted my students for their leadership roles and called them into those roles because my Crystal Ball told me they would perform spectacularly. Sometimes, a call to leadership is clear, just as that one was. But other times, it might not be.

With the Krannert conference story in mind, think a moment. Why are you reading this book?

If you wouldn't call yourself a "leader" but you're interested in helping others—serving them and solving problems—you are being called to leadership without realizing it, and your instinct led you here.

You expect something of yourself beyond the average. The question is, why? What values and ideals do you hold that make you want to serve others in this way? Where did you get those values and ideals?

If you do already consider yourself a leader, think about how you were first called into leadership. What problems did you step up to solve? What people did you take initiative to serve? Did someone ask it of you or appoint you, or did you volunteer?

How did it feel? Were you scared? Excited? Unsure? Even possibly unwilling? Maybe all at once? Were you confident you had solutions, or did you feel excitement at working to find them?

You might even remember the exact time and place when you realized, "This is leadership, and I'm the one who is leading!"

Knowing the way emerging leaders are called into leadership is important because it defines how they see expectations of themselves. If you understand how they were called to lead, you can show them what you see. You can also use these types of situations to help them to expect more of themselves.

According to Growing Leaders,[16] leaders are usually called into leadership in one of four ways. They are:

1. Positioned
2. Gifted
3. Summoned
4. Situated

Let's look at these situations in a little more detail to help you understand your own Chosen (and maybe even yourself) a little better.

---

16 Growing Leaders, *Habitudes Intensive* (Peachtree, GA: Growing Leaders, 2015)

Positioned Leaders

Some people are **positioned** to lead—they receive positions of leadership or responsibility. This can happen as early as preschool. One evening at the dinner table, my daughter could barely wait to tell us that she would be the "weather reporter" in her preschool class the next morning. My son had a similar experience with being the "mail helper" in his elementary classroom. He had the ever-important job of getting messages from his teacher to the school office.

Do you remember being the line leader or getting to change the calendar in your early school years? This is a very simple example of being positioned for leadership. As previously mentioned, positioned leaders have an official role that gives them some authority or responsibility for a particular task, location, or another area of oversight. Early in life, these positions are often assigned. Later, as the leader matures, he or she may elect or choose the position.

In your mentoring role, you have probably positioned others to lead. I think about my friend, Amy, who I knew would be a fantastic small group leader but didn't have the confidence to step into the role. I asked her to be in my group and serve as my sidekick. In this role, she bought everyone books, organized the snack schedule, sent notes of encouragement to group members on my behalf, etc. She was a fantastic sidekick, and I'll admit that I enjoyed handing those responsibilities to her. I saw her confidence in the role grow over the first year we were in a group together. That was encouraging, as I had more plans for her.

At the start of the second year of our group, I was called away on business for a week and needed someone to lead the group while I was gone. I called Amy and asked her to meet me for coffee, over which I asked her to lead the group the following week. She reluctantly agreed. I gave her the material, offered some suggestions, coached her through the material, and boosted her confidence.

Prior to taking over, she called me several times to ask questions and gain confidence that she was doing everything right. After her leadership, several members of the group contacted me to tell me what a great job she had done, and I encouraged them to be sure to contact her and sing her praises.

The next time I saw Amy, she was beaming. She admitted she had been very nervous and that she would have done some things differently in hindsight, but she felt very good about what she had been able to do. We changed her title from "sidekick" to co-facilitator that day, and the following year she began leading a group of her own. She has now served as the leader of the small group ministry for many years. Amy rose to the occasion once she was "tricked" into assuming a position.

Gifted Leaders

Some leaders are **gifted** to lead. You know them—they are the natural leaders whom others look to for leadership. They may not hold a position, but others respect and lean on their skills, knowledge, and temperament, especially when the going gets tough.

I used the example of my student Chase as a dispositional leader, and he would also fit into this category. Here's another example.

Samantha is gifted to lead and always has been. First off, she simply *looks* like a leader. She is strikingly tall but not intimidating due to her wide smile and kind eyes. But looks are just the beginning. Not only is she beautiful, but she also is highly intelligent, others-focused, and a forward thinker. Just before graduating as a doctor of pharmacy, she accepted a position to work at a nationwide hospital in her home state. It wasn't her first choice, but after talking with her about the position, the level of responsibility, and the fact that she would have the ability to teach, I knew it would be a perfect position for her. Not only would she be working in one of the nation's highest impact medical arenas, but she would also have the chance to use her skills and gifts to teach others. I'm sure the hiring team saw the qualities that make her a gifted leader and have positioned her well to use her entire repertoire of gifts and abilities. I can't wait to see the impact she'll have!

Summoned Leaders

Some leaders are **summoned** to lead. This "summoning" begins with an external problem that brings about an internal process.

For example, I myself was summoned to lead in one particular situation.

My mom is a domestic goddess. While I was growing up, she was the 80s version of Grub Hub, Uber, Merry Maids, and drop-off laundry service all rolled into one. I have no idea how she did it, but I never encountered an unwashed uniform or an unmade meal, and I was never late to a practice. And did I mention that our home was spotless? She was amazing—and still is.

When I was a sophomore in high school, she began suffering from severe panic attacks. I remember leaving for school one day as she was having one of her first attacks. I'd never seen anything like it before, and it was during the early stages of understanding anxiety disorders, so I didn't know what to think. I came home from school and practice that same day to find her asleep in bed. She'd had a very rough day, and after taking some prescribed medication to help calm her, she had finally fallen asleep. Little did we know that the medication would make her unable to function over the next several days.

Our usual smooth-running household came to a screeching halt. No one was preparing meals, laundry was piling up, and toilets needed to be cleaned. We had a problem. My dad, brothers, and I were all very busy, and we hadn't allowed any time in our schedules for these tasks. Not to mention the fact that, quite frankly, we didn't know how to do some of them.

But no one else was going to do it. The situation required my teenage brothers and me to step up and help solve the problem. We knew out of love and care for our mother and family that we needed to help in whatever way we could. (The fact that we appreciated clean underwear and good food had something to do with it, too.)

Perhaps you have been summoned to lead. What is your story? Perhaps you know others who have had such an experience. What is their story? What emerging leaders do you currently know who have been summoned to lead? Watch for them. They are the ones that need you to come alongside them most. Summoned leaders often don't know how to do the thing they are asked to do, and they can feel overwhelmed. They need their mentor to be there with them, offering support and a boost of confidence here and there as they navigate their challenges.

Situated Leaders

Situated leaders consist of two types of leaders: habitual leaders and situational leaders.

The easiest to spot are the habitual leaders, which comprise about 10-15 percent of leaders. These people take charge wherever they go. They almost can't help it. If they don't want to lead, they have to bite their tongues and sit on their hands. You may be one of them. I've learned in my more mature years that if I don't "want to be the change I want to see," then I need to keep my mouth shut and let others lead.

The other type of situated leader, the situational leader, is more difficult to spot. This is a leader who, encountering the right situation that matches their gifts and strengths, steps into that leadership confidently.

One of my dearest friends, Judy, is a retired high school guidance counselor who has helped thousands of students and families over the years. Judy keeps a pulse on the high school counseling world and serves as a resource for many, including me, with both challenge and support when needed.

I recently learned that Judy volunteers her time for multiple high schools to help with senior audits, making sure seniors have met the requirements for graduation. In this role, she serves as a situational leader. She has encountered the right situation and has matched her strengths, ability, and passion to it so she can lead with confidence in the audit process. Yet in other situations, Judy might not want to lead. Her decision depends on the situation and her ability to meet its specific demands.

Exercise: Define Your Chosen's Calling

After reading the previous examples and definitions of the types of calls to leadership, do a little work with your Chosen and learn more about how they were specifically called to lead—to solve the problem and/or serve the people they did, even if they didn't recognize it as leadership at the time.

Part 1: Group and Assess Them

Once you have more information, start putting them into their groups.

Those I know who are Positioned Leaders:

1. _____
2. _____
3. _____
4. _____
5. _____

Those I know who are Gifted Leaders:

1. _____
2. _____
3. _____
4. _____
5. _____

Those I know who are Summoned Leaders:

1. _____
2. _____
3. _____
4. _____
5. _____

Those I know who are Situated Leaders (note whether they are habitual or situational):

1. _____
2. _____
3. _____
4. _____
5. _____

Questions to Discuss

Why were they called into these particular situations? Ask some more questions:

- How did their passions factor in? Did they discover any new passions while they were in the situation?
- Why did they choose to solve that particular problem? How did they feel about it?
- What skills did they use to solve it?
- What would they have done differently? Why?
- What did they discover about themselves that they didn't know?
- What did they learn from the situation?
- How can they translate that experience into greater development for themselves—what areas/fields/groups do they want to work in/solve problems in/be part of?

Their vision will help you understand where they're coming from and why. Also, by the type of calling, you can gauge a little about their leadership style in general and how you would approach them to define expectations.

Think back to Chase. As a gifted leader, he was called to lead because people naturally sensed and respected his knowledge and insight and looked to him for leadership. At some points, he might have been called to leadership as a summoned leader, in situations where he didn't necessarily have the skills but was willing to step up to the plate to learn more and help his team succeed. Someone could even ask him to take a leadership position. But out of those, in which type of situation would he be most comfortable, demonstrate the most confidence, perform best, and be happiest?

What contributions do your Chosen want to make—but also how? This defines their expectations of themselves.

You may have to push someone like Chase or Amy out of their comfort zone in some cases, but you want to be aware of how to approach those situations based on the person's natural inclination.

Part 2: Decide Where to Take Their Calling

Now that you know why and how they were called to leadership, where should they take it? What do they want to see happen? What's their vision? What are their core values?

Have your mentee develop a statement for themselves based on their fundamental values.

"I was called into leadership by _____ .
The reason I chose to help was because I wanted to see _____ happen. Now that I have an idea of my skills and values, what I really want to do is use them to _____. To do that, I need to develop in the area(s) of _____."

This can add to their three spheres assessment to help you focus their development within their areas of passion and interest.

CHAPTER 5

Plan

"There are dreamers and there are planners; the planners make their dreams come true."

—EDWIN LOUIS COLE

Set and Achieve Expectations Together

Did you know that there are an estimated 12,386,344 possible plays to every baseball game?

My son, Noah, loves baseball and has been blessed to play for Coach Shambaugh, who lives and breathes baseball. Coach Shambaugh has coached the game for over thirty-five years, and I think he's played out the scenario of all 12,386,344 possible plays in a game.

When Noah started playing for Coach Shambaugh, he was in a hitting slump. Noah will probably never be a big-time hitter; that's not his strength. But Coach Shambaugh, with his Crystal Ball, saw Noah for who he is and what he brings to the field.

He saw where he could take Noah in two weeks and in two years, and he had an immaculate, detailed plan for how to get him there. It's tried and true.

Coach Shambaugh wasn't trying to shape Noah into a "big gun" hitter for the team. However, you can't score runs and win at baseball without getting on base. So, Noah's job is to get on base. That's his intention every time he's at bat. And he has learned the different strategies for accomplishing his goal. Many times, he's not the prettiest at bat, but he knows he's accomplished his intention if he ends up on base.

Working with Coach Shambaugh, Noah knew his overall goals and achievement markers in every aspect of the game and was involved in creating his plan to get there. This ownership has taken Noah's love for the game and skyrocketed it into passion. He knows his level of success is up to him, but he has a mentor who constantly challenges and supports him. Best of all, both Noah and Coach Shambaugh worked together to create and achieve the plan.

Base the Plan on Your Chosen's Values

There's an old saying that weaknesses are really just strengths applied in an unproductive way. Sometimes a plan has to help your Chosen stop using a strength in a way that isn't productive and turn it toward a different goal that will help the bigger picture. Since strengths come from values, that isn't always a straightforward thought process.

Here's an example from one of my colleagues who managed a team of editors. One of her best editors, Denise, was extremely perfectionistic about her editorial work, making her an excellent editor. However, she almost never met her deadlines, and she made a lot of unnecessary changes on printer proofs, which was costly. Denise's one-dimensional perfectionism, applied only to one part of her job, magnified her editing ability at the expense of meeting deadlines and keeping within a printing budget.

Her manager could have just sent Denise to project-management training or some other skills-building program. However, Denise had no passion for scheduling, and project management wasn't her area of strength. In fact, those kinds of tasks deflated her motivation. Denise also didn't want to be a supervisor or move to a higher rank, so the idea of that wouldn't motivate her, either.

However, her manager knew Denise enjoyed contributing to her team and mentoring other editors and that she also didn't like being late on projects, feeling like she had let her clients and teammates down. Her people skills and passion for excellent editing created a great deal of potential for her to serve her team in a greater capacity as an informal, dispositional leader and especially as a quality assurance expert.

To help Denise address her weakness in a way that would allow her skills to shine, her manager worked with her to set new goals. Denise would start considering budget and deadline as part of her main priorities. Now she not only had to consider the quality assurance in the editorial part of the project, but she also had to track and score herself on whether she met her project milestones and deadlines. If a project didn't meet its deadlines and stay within its print budget, it couldn't be considered as having met all of the expectations.

At first, Denise balked, believing success in this new context was impossible. After all, she had tried so hard to meet schedules but never could. However, her manager then challenged Denise to help create an editorial system where she could be sure she was upholding the desired editorial quality standards yet become much more efficient. Now Denise could put her skills to work in a different way, guided by the goals of this special project.

Working together, the two created a set of editorial quality criteria they could both agree on. They then worked through a new process to set limits on the kinds of changes that should be made at different editorial stages and which could be sacrificed at what point to meet the other goals of budget and deadline. Now Denise's goal was to catch things much earlier in the process and prioritize changes made for clarity and accuracy over others that didn't achieve either. Suddenly, with this system, which Denise herself helped build, her other "impossible" goals seemed much more possible.

The system satisfied her perfectionism and allowed her to speed up her work significantly. Her perfectionism no longer nagged her about checking for every type of error at every stage—those questions had already been answered upfront within the process guidelines that she herself had helped create. The bonus was that her meticulous attention to detail was embedded in the procedures that the rest of her team could now also follow and learn from—benefiting everyone. She was now far less stressed out about deadlines and budget goals and had more time to contribute her considerable skills and experience toward mentoring her less experienced teammates.

The plan didn't work on Denise's weaknesses by setting a goal for her to develop more in that area—it set a goal within her strengths in a way that would offset her weakness. She wasn't trying to become an expert scheduler; she was becoming a more efficient editor. She was challenged to use her strengths to determine how to meet her quality goals within the desired timeframes.

A Good Plan Creates Motivation

Benjamin Franklin said, "If you fail to plan, you are planning to fail." Often, the reason mentors fail is because they want to help others but don't have a clear set of goals for doing so. Without an action plan, it's difficult to keep on track, know how the Chosen is improving, or see where they need more help.

The plan itself creates part of the motivation. Even if you have a goal, if your Chosen doesn't see the clear steps to get there, or if they feel the end goal is just not achievable, they won't be motivated to achieve it. In fact, the end result might be demotivating, which is what you don't want.

In the preceding examples, each coach didn't just give his or her Chosen a pep talk and let them go keep trying to do their thing. They had not just a goal but also a clear framework for improvement. They both worked with their mentees to identify the achievable goals and outline their respective plans to reach them. Each plan was individually tailored to the person's situation, including their specific skills, strengths, weaknesses, and values/motivators. There is no "one size fits all" plan, even for people trying to develop the same skill or quality. The plan is based on the person.

It's important to make sure your plan includes the right elements to both motivate and develop your Chosen.

Steps to Create a Development Action Plan

The best way to avoid challenges and problems along the journey is to develop an action plan with your Chosen.

As you probably noted in the two examples above, an action plan is a checklist for the steps or tasks to be completed to achieve the development-related goals your emerging leader has set. This may be a new concept for them. Be patient. They will create a majority of the plan themselves, but they'll need time to think and adjust their goals as they learn more about their own values and true priorities.

As with my son Noah's batting situation, having an action plan will give you a clear direction. It's important that you have your Chosen put their goals in writing. Larger goals need to be broken into smaller steps that all lead to the larger goal. Things that aren't written down have a way of getting hazy and morphing into other things as we move through our daily activities. Suddenly we're not quite sure what we were trying to do or whether we're on the same wavelength. The written plan is a reference that will keep everyone on track.

It's also important to note that your emerging leader needs to see why a goal is important and how it can be achieved without sacrificing their other values, or he or she won't really want to achieve it. Denise, the editor, was motivated by quality standards but also by helping her team. Her goal of helping her team was her motivator for accepting that she needed development to meet budget and deadline goals. While Denise's goal wasn't quite the same as her manager's, her manager understood and valued Denise, saw where their two goals intersected, and was able to coach her effectively.

Ensuring the plan reflects your Chosen's own values and authentic self will help motivate them and increase their commitment. Priorities will become clearer, and you will have clear metrics that allow you to track progress. It's not difficult; the following are a few simple but very important steps and a sample template to get you started.

1. **Define your end goal using SMART goals criteria.**

    Each goal, including your end goal, should meet the SMART criteria—in other words, make sure it is:

    Specific: Well-defined and clear vs. general.

Measurable: Include measurement to track progress. For instance, dates by which something should be achieved, or doing X a specific number of times or to a specific standard of quality, etc. Even the goal of being able to do X without anxiety is a measurable goal—you can know when you're anxious or not, so you should know when you've achieved it.

Attainable: Realistic and achievable. Make sure your goal is within your means while still being challenging. You may have a goal to make $60K by next week, and that might be realistic for you. However, for most of us, it's not. You might also have a goal to fly by jumping into the air and flapping your arms, but that goal is probably not achievable.

Relevant: Does it align with your Chosen's other goals and the overarching plan? How does it fall within your Chosen's existing passions, values, and motivators?

Timely: It has a due date. Otherwise, it doesn't feel like a priority.

2. **List the steps to be followed.**

    The end goal is clear. What exactly needs to be done to realize it? Create a list of all the tasks to be performed and who is responsible. These specific tasks can also be SMART goals, though they'll usually be smaller and more incremental than the end goal.

3. **Prioritize tasks and add deadlines.**

    Reorganize the list by priority. Add deadlines and make sure they are realistic for the emerging leader. If he or she feels overwhelmed, the plan will become demotivating.

4. **Set milestones.**

    Think of milestones and mini goals leading up to the main goal. The advantage of achieving milestones is that they give something to look forward to and a way to stay motivated. Start from the end goal and work backward to set milestones.

    What does a milestone look like? It is simply a timeframe by which a certain set of something should be achieved. For instance, your Chosen could be trying to make specific connections within a field of interest to improve their networking. If they have a set of tasks or mini-goals related to finding those individuals and making those connections, they could set a milestone by which they will have developed five new connections and make sure all their relevant tasks and/or mini-goals fall within that timeframe.

5. **Identify resources needed.**

    It is crucial to have all the necessary resources at hand to complete the tasks or have a plan to acquire them. Resources can include anything that supports the task/goal—money, allotted time, knowledge, even people to network with. You might also include a budget here and how those funds will be acquired.

6. **Visualize your action plan.**

    Have your emerging leader create something that can be easily understood and seen. If they are a visual thinker, have them keep their plan somewhere easy to glance at, such as a whiteboard in their home office or in another prominent spot.

7. **Monitor, evaluate, and update.**

    Talk to your Chosen frequently to evaluate their progress. This step also helps bring out the tasks that are pending or delayed and will allow you to find suitable solutions. Update the action plan together accordingly.

8. **Reward your emerging leader (and yourself) as they complete major milestones.**

    What are the best rewards? That's up to you both! Define them and give yourself something to look forward to. This step may affect your budget, so plan accordingly.

Exercise: Create an Action Plan for Your Chosen

Now that you know how to create a framework to develop your Chosen, it's time for you to take action with one of them to put your knowledge into practice. Based on the qualities and skills you've both agreed are most important to reach All-Star level, use the SMART goals method to create the plan for their development.

Two Things to Remember When Creating an Action Plan

To create a successful plan, it's important to keep two things in mind.

1. Your plan doesn't have to be "perfect." There's no such thing as a perfect anything. Plus, "perfection" is a sliding scale. It's subjective. Your goal isn't to put together a perfect plan. It's to develop your Chosen. Much of the plan is going to be based on what and how they learn. What you start with may not be what you end up with, depending on what they learn about themselves, how they prefer to learn, and what you yourself learn about how they handle the above.

Coaches don't set a specific plan that never changes. They evaluate not only their mentee but also their own way of teaching that person. If the person is having trouble in some way, it might be time to adjust the teaching method. The key is to keep the end goal in mind.

2. Your Chosen should be deeply involved in all steps of the creation process so that it is based on their own values, priorities, and skills/capabilities.

Think back to Noah. He didn't have the natural talent to become an All-Star hitter, and if Coach Shambaugh had set that goal for him, it would have felt impossible—which would have been demotivating.

But Noah's goal was reachable. If he could get on base every time, he'd still be helping his team. That goal made him more valuable within the team context because it wasn't up to just Noah by himself to score points. The whole team was working together to do that. Knowing he could improve that skill to help his team kept the expectations smart—the goal was achievable—which kept him motivated. Coach Shambaugh showed Noah how he could contribute to the big picture, and Noah responded by stepping up to the task. The key was to find the right focus for the goal, based on his individual values and abilities.

Denise's manager was able to motivate her to set the goal by showing her how it would solve some of Denise's pain points—stress at not meeting deadlines and at letting her teammates down when her projects were delayed. Once Denise saw the way the plan would benefit her, she was fully engaged in it. When you are flexible where needed and include your Chosen in the planning process, you will have a far greater chance of succeeding.

Once you have your plan, what next? It's time to put them in the driver's seat and take your place as copilot.

Sample Action Plan

MENTEE ACTION PLAN	
Mentee Name:	Competency to be developed:

DISCOVER

Describe the situation where the mentee demonstrated leadership:

S: Situation _____

T: Task _____

A: Action _____

R: Result _____

DEVELOP

(Working with mentee) Set development goals that are focused, realistic, and tied to the mentee's long-term goals. Effective goals should be SMART:

S: Specific

M: Measurable

A: Achievable

R: Results-oriented

T: Time-based

Focus on competencies within the three spheres: power skills, character, and positive psychology. Build on their strengths as well as weaknesses. Look for growth, and learn by doing as well as observing and listening. Remember to expose them to levels of excellence within this competency.

Competency Details: What specific skill(s) need(s) development?	Learning Activities: What action(s) will we take to develop this area?	Beginning/ Ending Dates: When will each activity start/finish?	Observable Development: What specific new/ improved behaviors will indicate development?	Success: How will we know we've fully achieved the goal?

DEPLOY

Based on the mentee's values, how and where will they deploy their new skill(s) for the greatest impact?

CHAPTER 6

Guide

"The future depends on what you do today."
—GANDHI

The cold, driving rain was blowing in sideways sheets. It was a miserable, early spring day, with a sky that didn't live up to the promising forecast. My daughter, Sarah, and I sat in the car and talked through her plan for the upcoming track meet. She would need to do her best to stay dry and warm. She had seen some early success in the hurdles and high jump throughout the spring and had good intentions for the county-wide meet.

Within the first twenty minutes of the meet, we were soaked to the core, but after a spring of cancellations due to the pandemic and weather, everyone was working to make the county-wide track meet happen. I stood at the finish line, looking up the track at my daughter as she was preparing to run the 100-meter hurdles. Her entire body was shaking and shivering in the blasting wind as she stood at the starting line. The track conditions were horrible, and I prayed that everyone would safely run the race.

The gun went off and the race began. I breathed a sigh of relief as everyone safely crossed the finish line. Sarah did not place well enough to make it to the finals. We bundled her up and moved to the high-jump pit to focus on her next event.

The high jump was already underway, and Sarah quickly and intelligently made her first jump. I encouraged her to take as many jumps as she could early since she was still warmed up from running the hurdles. On her first jumps, she focused on clearing the height on her first attempt and getting as comfortable as possible with the ever-changing weather conditions. Thankfully, it had quit raining, and the wind had subsided a little. As the approach surface dried, jumping conditions improved. The competition progressed until two competitors remained—Sarah and another young woman.

With the bar height increasing and conditions changing, Sarah's jump strategy now had to change, too. Her competitor had cleared the present height on her first attempt. It was now Sarah's first attempt. She approached a little slowly and gave it a good try but missed. She was now in a "come from behind" position.

I called her to the fence, and we talked through the last jump. She knew she'd approached too slowly, and I could see the "I'm not coming from behind" look in her eyes. I encouraged her to run the length of the football field to get her muscles nice and warm. It had been quite some time since she was warm from her hurdle race.

She left the fence, and my husband looked at me and asked, "Do you think she'll clear it?" I answered with a shrug of my shoulders. I know Sarah isn't highly competitive. She likes to win but isn't necessarily driven to do so. So, as she ran the football field, I had to refocus how I would coach her through the next few jumps.

Sarah is very smart, articulate, and detailed, all qualities that had made her a successful hurdler and high jumper in her early track career. I knew I had to stick with the mechanics of jumping rather than on her drive to win.

When she returned from her football-field run, the official called her name to make her second attempt. I felt she was still a little out of breath and should wait a little longer, but she made her second attempt anyway. Another miss. It was now do-or-die.

I called her to the fence again. We talked through every intricate detail of her approach and jump. Then I had her visualize herself clearing that height. When she opened her eyes, I gave her the biggest smile I could muster, told her to jog back to the pit "feeling light" and clear this height. Off she went.

She approached her starting mark and gave the official an affirmative nod. Her approach looked fantastic, her plant foot was firm, her arm drive into her jump was strong, and she worked her body over the bar with the style of a well-fitted glove—not too much or too little space between her body and the bar. She cleared and was still in the competition! Her competitor, after watching the jump, knew it was "game on."

Sarah came to the fence with a huge smile on her face and a "that felt good" on her lips. However, based on misses, she was still behind. She knew it, and we talked through it. She was warm and riding high on momentum, so I encouraged her to make her first jump at the new height fairly quickly. She jogged with a pep in her step over to the official and requested to jump.

The official granted her jump request, so she approached her starting mark, collected her thoughts, and envisioned herself clearing the bar. As she was preparing mentally, the sun peeked from behind the rain clouds. She began with another strong approach;

she drove the heel of her plant foot into the ground, drove her arms to the sky, and then worked every single part of her body, starting with her head, then shoulders, her lower back, then hips, then knees and finally her heels over the bar. She had cleared the new height on her first attempt, and it was a thing of beauty.

We could sense each other's relief as she approached the fence, and she had a huge smile on her face. The pressure was now on her competitor. She wrapped herself in a dry blanket and a cloak of appropriate confidence. Now we just had to watch as her competitor jumped.

The young lady began her first approach, jumped, and clipped the bar with her heels. Miss #1. We knew Sarah was sitting in a nice potential finishing position, but her competitor had just made a fantastic attempt, and we knew with just a little tweaking on her part she could easily clear this height. Sarah was momentarily distracted by cheering for her teammates who were running in a relay past our perch at the fence. The relay ended, and we refocused on the high jump pit. Her competitor took her second jump: again a great attempt, but a miss. We were breathing easier.

The track meet was concluding, so many were gathering at the high jump area. It had been a long and hard-fought battle that would come down to one last jump. Sarah's competitor made her final approach and missed her third attempt. The young lady had just run out of steam after a long evening and a fantastic competition. They both had much to be proud of as they shook hands. Sarah, the youngest competitor in the competition, had won.

On the drive home, we talked about her two events that evening. She had good intentions in the hurdles but didn't run the race intentionally. She had the same thoughts with the high jump but acted intentionally on every step in the process with a much better outcome. The starkly different results showed the importance of not only the intention to win but also the intention and ability to put all the small pieces together to make the larger goal.

The Role of a Guide

This is going to sound funny, but when I think of coaching and mentoring, bowling comes to mind. Not just bowling—but those inflatable gutter guards they use for young bowlers so that their bowling ball doesn't go into the gutter.

That's kind of what a coach does: they keep their Chosen focused on the end goal and out of the gutter. They may even "bump" their Chosen back into proper position as needed. Your emerging leader doesn't want to go into the gutter, and if that happens enough times, they lose confidence in their abilities. While they're learning the mechanics of when to let go of the ball, how to aim and focus, and how to improve their form, they don't need to worry about where the gutter is. They just need to build their confidence.

After they reach a certain stage of skill, they won't need the gutter guards anymore. They now know how to bowl well enough and have built their confidence levels so that even if their ball does go into the gutter, it won't affect their overall game enough to make a difference. They can take a few misses in stride.

Coaching vs. Mentoring

When I use the term "coach," an athletic coach may come to mind, but the definition of coaching involves much more than that. Coaching is partnering

> *Coaching is partnering with another in a thought-provoking, creative process that inspires them to maximize their personal and professional potential.*

with another in a thought-provoking, creative process that inspires them to maximize their personal and professional potential.

Coaching and mentoring are first cousins. In your mentoring process, you will dance between coaching and mentoring. Coaching is less directive, gives less instruction, and allows the emerging leader to drive the process.

In the graphic, "Coaching Continuum," note that there are different kinds of interaction for different results.

To compare coaching and mentoring, it's helpful to look at them in the context of types of coaching, or as a "continuum." Coaching is shorter-term, involves different types of feedback, and is driven by the coach, while the mentoring process is more directive and explicit in helping assess progress.[17]

In my experience, coaching and mentoring often happen hand in hand. In other words, they're not necessarily exclusive. Even athletic coaches, who are usually focused on the performance for the sport at hand, can also perform some broader mentoring activities with their athletes when needed. Just look at Coach Bauer's goal-setting method, which she taught her athletes. That applies to other things besides sports.

The beauty of coaching is that you are not responsible for meeting the goal. Your role as coach is to be a "guide on the side," asking the right questions to inspire learning and offering accountability and encouragement.

---

17 Kriss Akabusi, "Coaching and Mentoring: What's the Difference?" accessed April 2, 2022, https://www.akabusi.com/latest-news/2016/12/15/coaching-and-mentoring-whats-the-difference

Coaching Continuum

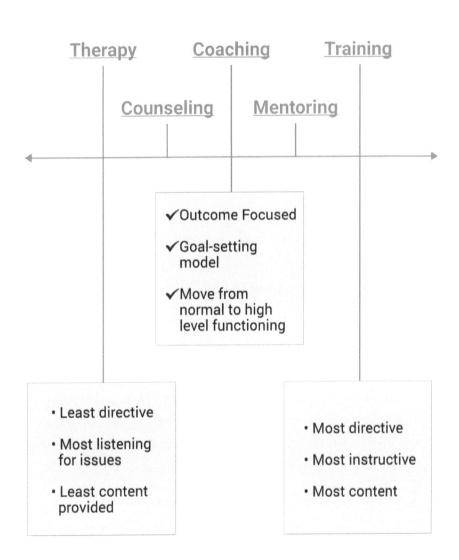

Coaching provides an extra edge for your emerging leader that they wouldn't have alone. It offers fresh perspective needed to take massive action. It's what sets the highest achievers apart from the rest of the pack. Coaches help create change and unlock peak performance. Coaches are trained to skyrocket us to new heights of performance by showing us what we're capable of when we remove limitations and move past our comfort zones. Coaches help us to set goals that align with our most important priorities and then create a plan to achieve them. Coaches help take others from average to All-Star!

But it doesn't really matter what you call it. To quote Nike, "Just Do it!"

Challenge. Support. Repeat to infinity.

The Top Ten Mistakes Coaches and Mentors Make

Worried about how to approach the relationship? Here's a list of the top ten mistakes mentors make.[18]

1. **Building a one-sided relationship.** A mentoring relationship should be a give and take in terms of communication, responsibility, commitment, etc. In the beginning, it may be more mentor-driven, but as the relationship and development progress, it will change, becoming more mentee-driven.

2. **Not defining the commitment.** Both people in the relationship need to be clear about what they plan to commit in terms of time, availability, and specific types of actions. For instance, if

---

18 "Top 10 Mentoring Mistakes to Avoid" Ten Thousand Coffees. February 8, 2021, https://www.tenthousandcoffees.com/blog/top-10-mentoring-mistakes-to-avoid/.

you plan on being more of a coach than a mentor, that needs to be clear. If you plan on helping the person develop a very specific skill set through dedicated training sessions, that needs to be clear.

3. **Not setting goals.** Failing to have SMART goals makes the relationship just another interaction. It might still be helpful, but it will not be as effective as having and meeting goals. Also, you can't track your progress without goals.

4. **Being critical instead of constructive.** It's tempting to focus only on all of the things your mentee isn't doing well, but if you dwell in this area, it will just alienate and demotivate them.

5. **Lacking flexibility.** Flexibility for a mentor can be tricky. You want to hold your mentee to high standards that appropriately drive development, yet you also need to adjust expectations, timelines, and standards when needed.

6. **Just telling your mentee what to do.** This goes back to the "stop giving advice" advice I gave you earlier. They need to develop their own problem-solving skills. You can help them figure out the problem, but they need to determine how to solve it.

7. **Talking too much.** If you're the only one doing the talking, they won't feel they're being heard, and they might feel the relationship is all about you. If you find yourself in this situation, challenge yourself to "WAIT." Ask yourself, "Why Am I Talking?"

8. **Not sharing enough.** It's important for mentors and coaches to show that we're real people. If you don't share enough of your own personal experience, mission, or values/goals, you won't be able to connect with your mentee at anything other than a

superficial level. They need to know you've failed, too, and that you've had times of despair or frustration.

9. **Knowing all the answers.** You might have an answer. But is it the right answer for that other person? It's important for mentors to be inquisitive about the unique process and the solution for that particular mentee rather than already "be there" in our minds. The mentee has to bring his or her own solution. You're just there to ask the right questions.

10. **Breaking trust.** If you break even small commitments, your mentee will start to doubt the relationship. Failing to show up for appointments, not following through on promises, or seeming only interested in the relationship for your own gain will create major trust issues and cause more harm than good.

Note that your mentee may not feel comfortable enough bringing any of the above to your attention. If they do, however, consider it a compliment—they value the relationship enough to provide their own honest feedback.

Word Choices Mean Everything

Sometimes, the difference between criticism and constructive feedback is just the words you choose.

How do these words make you feel when you hear them?

A. Critical/Negative Approach: (Thinking for Them)	B. Constructive/Positive Approach: (Encouraging Them to Think for Themselves)
You need to do X.	What are some options you could do?
You haven't been doing X, as you'd committed to do. That's really hurting you.	How often have you been doing X, as you'd committed to do? How do you feel that's affected your situation in general? What's getting in your way?
Your main problem is X.	What do you feel is the main thing that's holding you up? Are there alternatives? What if you do X instead of Y?
Your attitude is causing X problem for yourself.	What's your biggest current mental/emotional challenge? How is it affecting your situation? How do you feel you could address it?
If you keep doing X, you're going to ruin all your opportunities.	It looks like you've missed a few opportunities. What kinds of things do you think have prevented you from taking them?

Their answers to the questions in B are opportunities to offer additional suggestions from your own experience if they are faltering, but not as statements. They should be phrased as questions.

One element that gets in the way is something called the "arc of distortion." When you're saying things, they might be getting filtered through the receiver's assumptions, fears, and projections. Your intended meaning gets lost, and another takes its place. Communicating is vital—but you want to make sure your Chosen is getting the right message.

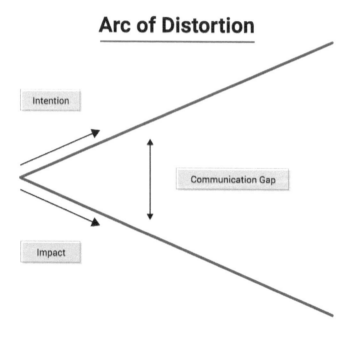

Interactions with your mentee depend heavily on the right kinds of communication—including knowing when to make suggestions and when to get your mentee to make their own suggestions. Much of mentoring and coaching is listening and asking the right questions.

Instead of, "It seems like you have a lot of negativity about that particular activity. Maybe you should start seeing a therapist or journaling to get all of that out," you could say, "I get what you're saying. It seems you have a lot of mental conflicts on that topic. That must be frustrating because those conflicts are obstacles that are getting in the way of your success." Note that the first statement is deflecting and offers a "quick fix" without empathy, while the second statement shows empathy and sums up the situation. After the second statement, you could go on to ask questions. "How have you tried to work around or through your internal obstacles? Do you feel your expectations of yourself in those situations are realistic? What underlying assumptions could you be making that could be hindering your progress? What might you try, knowing everything you know to this point?" At that point, if they're looking at an alternate plan, you can suggest resources, etc., if you know of them. "I think that's a great idea! I just read an awesome book about that if you want to check it out." Or, "Wow, that's an innovative approach. Do you need networking help in that area? I can check my contacts and see if there's anyone I could connect you with," etc.

They've found the potential solution—you're just providing resources.

When you're coaching for a specific result, you can provide positive feedback along with questions. "Your presentation was really great! You did X, Y, and Z very well. I did notice you having some trouble with W, though—what was going on there?" Again, turn it back to them. The key is to empathize rather than criticize—you're feeling their pain right along with them. That's part of what they need to know. You're not criticizing; you're empathizing and giving them emotional support as they seek solutions.

Keeping Your Mentee (and You!) Motivated

Mentoring relationships happen over long periods of time, so it's only natural that they'll ebb and flow like any other relationship. Sometimes it's great: sometimes it's not. That's normal, especially with longer-term mentoring relationships. (Remember—not every mentoring relationship lasts a year. You can have a coaching/mentoring relationship that lasts two months or two years [but that would be rare]. It depends on what you choose and how you decide to do it.)

In fact, according to Mentoring Complete, slumps often occur in the last months—especially at the nine-month mark. By this time, a natural shift occurs. "It's become more of a true relationship rather than a partnership where the mentor and mentoree are focusing on goals and objectives," they wrote.[19]

Part of your job as a mentor is to be a cheerleader. You need to show that the mentoring time is worth sticking to in the long run.

Here are three simple tips[20] to re-engage your mentee:

1. Send a quick encouragement text (or two or three). Everyone enjoys some encouragement!
2. Send a note about a random topic. Look for something that might be interesting to them. It might be a quote, an idea from a book, a funny meme, etc. Make it specific to their unique personality and focus areas. Let them know you're thinking about them.

---

[19] Mentoring Complete (2019). Mentoring 'Slumps'—How to Get Back on Track, retrieved March 10, 2022, https://www.get.mentoringcomplete.com/blog/how-to-tackle-mentoring-slumps

[20] Adapted from "How to Motivate your Mentee to Keep Coming Back," https://www.pursuegod.org/how-to-motivate-your-mentee-to-keep-coming-back/

3. Do something fun. Mentoring isn't always about intentional conversations. Sometimes it's about just enjoying each other's company.

Keep track of your communications with your mentees and make sure you yourself don't drop off their radar. It's easy to get busy and forget to check in. Set a periodic reminder to do one of the above with your mentees each week, month, etc. What that looks like each time might be different; the key is to let them know they're important to you by staying in touch.

If you're feeling like the relationship is stagnating for you, try thinking about it in new ways. Mentoring Complete offers suggestions like changing your meeting venues, asking other mentoring pairs for tips, and having your mentee keep a journal of challenges and successes to discuss at the next meeting.[21] It's easy to forget to bring things up when you don't write them down, and they get lost amid all your other life activities.

Also, if the relationship is shifting near the end of the mentoring focus, that's usually a good sign that the mentoring part is decreasing to the point where eventually, you're just catching up as two people who enjoy each other's company, rather than talking about goals. That's what you're shooting for! Good mentoring relationships don't "end," they just transition to more peer-to-peer relationships. If you notice this, point it out with your mentee as something to celebrate, not worry about—and then figure out a fun way to celebrate it together.

---

21 Mentoring Complete (2019). "Mentoring Slumps: How to Get Back on Track" https://www.get.mentoringcomplete.com/blog/how-to-tackle-mentoring-slumps

Did I Do Something Wrong?

Sometimes, mentoring relationships encounter their own kinds of "breakups." This may or may not come with an explanation, but even so, it's not always clear whether you receive the whole story. People often don't want to share their personal information, or they feel uncomfortable voicing their concerns about something and instead choose to just disappear or fade slowly away despite your attempts to engage them.

If it's because they feel something about the relationship isn't working for them, but they lack the confidence to bring it up themselves, you can help create a safe space by consistently welcoming feedback and constructive criticism yourself.

Also, being attentive to your mentee and aware of these shifts in their attention from the beginning can help break the ice early so smaller issues don't go unrecognized and unaddressed. Be sincere and ask for honest feedback. "Is there anything you feel could be better about our interaction? What areas would you like me to work on as a mentor?" Better yet, provide them with a list of the common mentoring mistakes and ask them for feedback on how you're doing related to those. Tell them what you think your own weaknesses are in those areas, and ask them to let you know when you need to work on something.

You can rectify most mistakes or misunderstandings if you are sincere about the commitment and reinforce that their feedback helps you improve, too. This reinforces your own commitment.

Remember: It's Not Necessarily You

Keep in mind that sometimes the issues have nothing to do with what you're doing or not.

I'll never forget one of my students, Gina, approaching me after class looking like she was about to cry. One of the requirements for the Krannert Mentoring Program was a leadership class, for which their grade depended on how they engaged their own mentees.

Gina's mentee was a first-year student in their first semester of college. In general, first-year students fell into one of two buckets: Either they would hang on every word their mentor said, or they were so distracted they didn't even remember they had a mentor.

Gina's situation seemed to fall into the second category, and she quickly confided in me that she thought she was "doing it wrong" and would fail the course. I assured her that neither was likely, and we set up a time for her to visit me in my office later that day.

When we met later, Gina admitted that listening to the success stories the other students had been sharing in class had set her on edge. Her comments helped me realize we needed to share both success and "struggle" stories in class so that everyone could relate.

Gina's struggle was that her mentee wouldn't respond to any communications or take part in any of the activities we'd set up for the pairs. There were always a handful of mentors with this situation, so I did what I normally did in those circumstances, reaching out to the mentee myself via email to remind them that they had committed to the course and their mentor's grade partly depended on their participation. Yet in Gina's situation, even that didn't help. I finally submitted a notification to the Office of the Dean of Students, letting them know I was concerned about this student.

Several weeks passed, during which we paired Gina with another mentor who had two mentees, creating a group mentoring scenario so that Gina could still experience some success as we were waiting to hear about the other student. We finally learned that the student had been dealing with some mental health issues and had withdrawn from college. Gina hadn't done anything wrong—and later, she told me what a valuable lesson that entire experience had been.

"I learned that it's not about me; it's about the person I'm trying to help," she said. Though we never learned the whole story of that student's situation (and we pray it ended well), Gina had learned a valuable lesson.

What If I Have to End the Relationship?

It's rare, but it does happen. Sometimes a mentor may have to end a relationship for whatever reason.

However, it should go without saying that as a mentor, you're setting an example for your mentee. If you feel the relationship isn't working, it's your responsibility to voice your concerns and suggest alternatives. Only when you've exhausted all options for communication should you consider ending the relationship.

Most issues can be rectified with constructive criticism and communication. Here are some examples:

1. **They're asking more than you were prepared to give.** For instance, they seem to want you to devote more time to them or solve their problems for them. In cases like this, reinforce and clearly communicate the boundaries, kindly explaining what you will do and also why it's important for them to do what they need to do within the relationship.

2. **They aren't communicating with you or responding to your requests.** In this case, try setting an in-person meeting (or videoconference if you're not close by) with them. Priorities can shift when you are talking face to face—and it's easier to connect and get more into what is going on with them.

3. **They seem motivated in person but aren't following through on their goals.** Ask them to take a look at the goals with you and determine whether they're realistic based on what they've got going on right now. It's easy to decide what you're going to do without a clear idea of how much time and focus you'll have. When reality becomes clearer, goals need to shift, or they may feel so impossible that your mentee will abandon them—which is also abandoning themselves. It's much better to make smaller incremental progress than no progress at all.

If you've sincerely tried to address issues but the relationship still isn't working, try to take it in stride. In many cases, it's often really no one's fault. Maybe your personalities aren't quite the right fit, and they've found another person who is a better fit (or you've thought of someone to connect them with). That's actually great! They're learning more about their authentic selves. Or, maybe they've encountered a life situation that just isn't going to allow the mentoring relationship right now, such as in Gina's case. Or, perhaps you've had a major life change yourself—in which case, you owe it to your mentee to find him or her another coach/mentor if possible.

As a mentor, if you do feel you should end the relationship, doing so should always be considered with the best interests of both you and the mentee in mind. And it should always be a last resort after you've exhausted all other options.

It also should go without saying that if you do need to end the relationship, you should always provide an explanation. Never leave your mentee guessing. You chose them for a reason—breaking off the relationship incorrectly will give a negative signal that might harm their confidence, which could set them even further back in their development. Remember: you're always setting an example. Even at the end of the relationship, they need constructive feedback so they can make good decisions about finding and working with mentors in the future.

Exercise: Create a Coaching Framework for Working with Your Mentee

In the last chapter, you created a plan for developing your mentee, but how will you execute that plan? How often will you meet and discuss progress? How will you keep your mentee motivated and on track? How will you use your own strengths to be the "gutter guard" to keep your mentee's ball in the lane and knocking down pins?

Here's a set of questions to help you get started. Be sure to include your mentee in this part of the process.

1. What kind of coaching/mentoring is needed in this situation? Does the mentee need more coaching, more in-depth mentoring, skills training, or a mix? How will we regularly assess these guidelines and make sure they haven't changed?

2. Over how long of a period of time will we hold meetings—a month? A year? (It helps to decide this based on your decisions in #1; some things may only take a few weeks to develop, while others will take longer. Also, consider based on what you both are willing/able to commit to. You can even set a goal to assess within two months and see if you need to continue.)

3. How often will we meet? Will it be weekly, bi-weekly, monthly, etc.? How long will each meeting last?

4. How will we meet? Will it be in person? Via phone or videoconference?

5. What kinds of obstacles (time, logistics, etc.) might be an issue, and how can we work together to help ensure we stay on track and prevent them from derailing our progress together?

6. Are there any other ways in which we will communicate with each other despite formal meetings? What's acceptable in terms of contacting each other? Is it all right to text, email, etc., at any time, or are we setting parameters for that? What's a reasonable expectation for me to get back with you and you to get back with me?

7. How can I get feedback on my own skills/effectiveness as a coach/mentor? How can we create a safe space for you to give me feedback on how you feel the relationship is working and whether I could improve something?

8. What kinds of other fun activities can we do together aside from meetings? Keep those in mind as we continue our relationship.

9. Are there any other considerations we need to discuss to ensure this is an enjoyable, productive process for both of us?

"Excellence is never an accident. It is always a result of high intention, sincere effort, and intelligent execution; it represents the wise choice of many alternatives—choice, not chance, determines your destiny."

—ARISTOTLE

STEP 3

DEPLOY

CHAPTER 7

Instill

"We are what we repeatedly do.
Excellence, therefore, is not an act but a habit."
—ARISTOTLE

In one of my previous positions at Brightpoint University, the department where I worked was tasked with executing the president's vision for training and development. We were a fairly new team ourselves; my supervisor was new, and in addition to myself and another woman who had been on the team a while, we had just hired two new young trainers, Jason and Rob. Jason came from a real estate background and was new to training and development, and Rob was a recent college graduate, so both were inexperienced with the work.

Our group had already been working in this new focus area, and we had developed a structure and the starting curriculum. When Jason and Rob came in, we first had to train them so they could then train others. They started by taking direction from us. Then they got their feet under them, only requiring feedback on how they were doing. After about nine months to a year after they had started in their roles, we had a meeting in which suddenly, they took over points on the agenda and drove the conversation.

After the meeting, I looked at my supervisor and said, "You realize what just happened there, right?" And she just grinned and nodded.

These two young men, who just less than a year ago had been totally dependent on us to do their jobs, were now calling their own shots and making good decisions and suggestions for how the whole function could improve. It was amazing to see their development.

The Drive for Excellence

Nothing tells you you're on the right track like your mentee suddenly taking the wheel and driving the bus.

This is what you're shooting for—this is the reason to mentor people. You want to see them learn and then start owning their own "game," whatever that might be. They are able to see where to go, what to do—and most importantly, decide how. They're no longer waiting for suggestions or acknowledgment from you—they're making suggestions and showing leadership in their area.

Really, your whole goal is for them to get to the point where they don't need you. They're ready to jump out of the nest and take flight on their own wing power. And they're not only going to fly—they're going to fly with amazing grace and agility and go places you've never dreamt of.

But what takes them to that point?

When they see their own vision of excellence in fulfilling their purpose and goals, that will naturally start to happen.

To understand how that happens, let's take a quick look at what we've done to get where we are now.

So far, you've discovered your mentee, taken a good look at his/her skills, background, goals, and passions, and developed a plan to help them improve their skills in a way that motivates them to succeed, as well giving them the steps to do so. You've been right alongside them, helping support and guide them to stay on track as they've deployed their growing skills in a way that keeps the process moving forward and provides opportunities for them to stretch their wings.

Up till now, you've been the one guiding the expectation that they will be extraordinary.

As you've been discussing excellence together, hopefully, you've both defined excellence as part of the SMART metrics for their development plan—but now it's time for them to "own" that drive for excellence in their own ways. This is a key facet of leadership. Leaders help define and redefine excellence within their chosen areas of expertise. Now is the perfect time for them to work on personally internalizing that drive for excellence so that as they work to achieve their goals, they are continually motivated to learn and grow more each time—and to set higher goals.

To get your young leader started thinking in this way, they need to define what excellence means to them specifically and include it as part of their motivation for success. How do they feel when they've done an excellent job at something? What does real excellence look like?

What does "extraordinary" look like within their area of passion?

There's no fault in having pride in a job well done, or in one's work ethic for achievement, or in one's accomplishments in self-development, as long as that pride is balanced by the humility of knowing there's always more to learn and do to grow. It's time for your young leader to create and internalize their own standards and expectations of excellence so that it won't matter whether anyone else expects those things of them. When they do this, they'll just know how to set their bar higher for themselves than others would set it for them and naturally do so.

Teaching the Excellence Mindset

Excellence is an element of being extraordinary. How do we know excellence when we see it? How do we create it? How do we drive to have it? How do we make it a habit?
As coaches, how do we teach it?

Discover Examples of Excellence

I believe in intentionally exposing young leaders to excellence and calling it out when you see and experience it. So, what does that mean? Let me give you a few examples:

1. **Watch the Olympics.** Observe world-class competition and sportsmanship, watch the human-interest stories related to the Olympics, and discuss what elements elevate it to a level of excellence.

2. **Visit or discuss places of excellence with your mentee.** Depending on where you go, this one will cost you a little, but you can experience excellence firsthand. Take your mentee out to a restaurant that has excellent food and service and discuss it while you're there. Visit a local business with excellent products and talk to the salespeople about why they are of such high quality. With family members, a great option for both exposure to excellence and a great vacation at the same time is a trip to Disney. (Though you likely won't get to take non-family mentees to one of their theme parks unless you're attending a conference

or other event for work there, if they've already been there, you can ask them to recall the trip.) Disney focuses on and extensively trains its cast members on customer service excellence. What steps do they take to not just care for their guests but to create a magical (excellent) experience? Teaching your mentee to look at everything through these filters is an ideal way to get them learning without your being there all the time.

3. **Have your Chosen attend a collegiate or professional camp or clinic** so they can observe or experience their craft at the highest level. It may be intimidating, but it's important to expose your emerging leaders to excellence.

4. **Have your mentee research places of excellence.** This would be a great way to familiarize them with places like Disney without incurring the cost. A great research subject (besides Disney) is the Ritz Carlton. The Ritz offers the gold standard of exceptional customer service. Have your mentee give you their thoughts about the Ritz's Three Steps of Service. There are great case studies online describing excellent organizations and their philosophies and standards.

5. **Attend or observe professional performances or exhibitions together.** These should obviously be based on your Chosen's area of interest. If it's music, attend a concert or the philharmonic. If it's dance or theatre, attend a professional-level performance. If it's robotics, attend the state competition. If it's showing animals, attend a national show. If you don't live close by or aren't able to attend an event together, these don't have to be in person—find and watch a good professional presentation video if that works. Then meet and discuss what made the presentation excellent or not.

During discussions of these experiences, talk with your emerging leader about specifics, such as:

1. What does excellence look like in this setting? How can that translate to your life?

2. What does excellence sound like? How can you sound excellent?

3. How do leaders create excellence in this setting? How can you create excellence?

4. What other similar examples of excellence have you seen? Why are they excellent?

Ways to Develop Excellence

The old saying, "Practice makes perfect," is an old saying that is still consistently used because it's proven true in more cases than not.

When you think of ways to deploy your young leader, it's good to consider opportunities where they will practice and refine their ideas of excellence. Here are some ways to consider their opportunities for contribution.

Muscle Mastery

Sometimes, your young leader literally needs to practice, aside from being in opportunities where they're applying their skills publicly.

One of my all-time favorite young leaders is Kaitlyn Schleis. I first met Katie when she was a sophomore at Purdue University and was serving as an ambassador for the university as one of the All-American Marching Band's feature twirlers. Within a few months of our knowing her, she rose to the top feature twirler position as Purdue's Golden Girl. We had hired Katie to be my daughter's baton-twirling coach.

Katie quickly became a trusted coach and personal friend, and it's been a pleasure to watch her grow into a fabulous young woman. In 2019, we were blessed to watch Katie compete for and win the National Collegiate Twirling Championship.

A few weeks after her national championship victory, Katie came to our home for dinner and to give a baton lesson. During dinner, I asked Katie what her key was in pulling off such a flawless championship routine. She hesitated for a moment, thinking. Then she said, "I just practiced doing my routine correctly so many times that I couldn't do it wrong." Her answer was profound. I had heard of muscle memory, but she had trained her muscles, brain and all, to the level of muscle mastery. Not only was her answer pure excellence, but so was the muscle mastery concept, and her national championship performance.

Okay, this makes sense with baton twirling. But how about in business and other organizational settings?

"Muscle mastery" is a way to embed master skills. Leadership requires a lot of skills, including things such as making presentations, thinking on your feet, staying cool in difficult situations, and giving constructive criticism. Just because they don't necessarily require physical muscles doesn't mean you can't use the same concept. Your young leader can practice all of these by themselves or with others in role-playing situations and by putting themselves in situations where they will have to think on their feet—even physically.

For instance, to practice quick response and confidence, they could get involved in sports, martial arts, debate classes, or other types of situational training. They don't have to just wait for opportunities to practice their "muscle mastery" in relevant skill sets. Many types of skills transfer to different situations. Getting accustomed to criticism and improvement in sports translates to doing so in business settings, and learning to think on your feet in a martial art and respond to changing circumstances during sparring will build confidence and responsiveness in other settings, not just the martial art. Practicing presentations, public speaking, and even specific kinds of conversations, either alone or with a friend, will help your young leader improve in many different interpersonal areas.

10,000-Hour Rule

All right. How much practice does a person need?

The 10,000-Hour Rule, which is closely associated with pop psychology writer Malcolm Gladwell, holds that 10,000 hours of "deliberate" practice are needed to become world-class in any field.[22] This theory has been debated, but no matter what side of the debate you're on, it's obvious that developing excellence in any area takes a lot of practice; Gladwell explained that the 10,000 hours figure is just an average.

And it's not just practice—it has to be practiced **with both initial aptitude and also attention to excellence.** You can practice squeaky violin-playing for 10,000 hours, and you'll be excellent at playing a squeaky violin. But if you practice it with a drive for true standards of excellence, after 10,000 hours, you will be a world-class violinist. Here again, intention enters the equation.

Those who practice with the intention to improve listen for where they need to improve. It's not just what you practice but also how. How you practice is how you will perform.

You will probably not see your emerging leader through 10,000 hours of development, but it's important to encourage them to think in this way in their drive toward excellence.

---

22 Malcolm Gladwell, "Complexity and the Ten-Thousand Hour Rule," *The New Yorker*, August 21, 2013, https://www.newyorker.com/sports/sporting-scene/complexity-and-the-ten-thousand-hour-rule/.

String Successful Skills Together

One thing I've learned through my athletic and coaching career is the concept of gaining momentum by stringing together success skills. My high-jump coach, Coach Pearson, was the first to introduce this concept to me, and I use the concept almost every day. It is an athletic concept that translates to just about every aspect of life—including how I coached my own daughter, Sarah, in her high-jump event.

From a high-jump perspective, it contained three elements:

Phase 1: The Approach

The first skill needed for a successful jump was the perfect approach. The approach had to be practiced to the point that it was consistently excellent. Then, measurements were made so we would know the exact starting point of the approach. Once the approach began, we had to know the different paces of the different phases of the approach. It would start with the slight prance. Think of a horse prancing with high-bent knees. Our mindset during this phase had to be "light" in preparation to clear the bar. About midway through the approach, we had to change from "light" to gaining speed. This was in preparation for our foot plant that would translate our horizontal energy into vertical energy. The key with our approach, too, was that if our approach wasn't consistent or didn't feel right, we were not to make the jump. We had to be able to approach the jump without hesitation.

Phase 2: The Foot Plant

After the approach came the foot plant. The first key was consistent foot placement near the stanchion and parallel to the bar. Once the placement was there, the next key was the exaggerated planting of our heel into the ground. This was the key to translating our speed (horizontal energy) into height (vertical energy). Just after the foot plant came the driving of the opposite knee and arms straight up into the air. Every part of the body was driving high.

Phase 3: Working Over the Bar

At the height of our jump is when the third phase of the approach took shape. We called this "working over the bar." Our heads and bodies rotated a quarter turn. Our head "flicked" back, and our front arm straightened to allow the top third of our body to clear the bar. Once our head and shoulders cleared, we drove our hips to the sky and finished by quickly bringing our chin to our chest, which provided the kick of the feet to successfully clear the bar.

Now, how does that translate into a business setting?

The phases translate into three specific stages in general for this particular goal. These three stages create a process that, when put together in the correct way each time, build on each other's success to achieve the goal.

Let's look at it in reverse. If you don't have a good approach, you have to work a lot harder to recover and have a good foot plant—but even then, you may not have built up the momentum needed to get over the bar. And if you don't have a good foot plant, you're not going to come from an optimum place and have the right tension in your spring to get over the bar. Finally, if you do the first two steps but you aren't able to perform the bodily calculations to clear the bar, you're still not going to achieve the goal.

All three things are important, and done successfully, they build on each other, stacking their individual positive achievements to achieve the goal.

With that in mind, you can break goals into relevant skill sets and achievements to see how they all work together and build toward success. Here are two examples:

Example 1: Sales presentation. This can be broken down into several big-picture stages: research, creating the presentation, making the pitch, and closing the deal. If your research isn't good, you won't know the client's situation well enough to recommend the right product or service solution. If you don't create an excellent presentation, you won't be able to make it well. Even if you've written an excellent presentation, you still have to be able to give it in a clear, engaging way and read the room to field objections, or you won't achieve the next stage. And finally, if you've done a great job at all the previous things but you didn't use your skills to follow up and close the deal effectively, none of the other aspects matter. In addition, each of these stages can be broken down into smaller increments, too. For instance, when making the presentation, you have your introduction, your persuasive argument, your pitch, your Q&A session, and your closing. Each of these has to accomplish a certain thing, or the next steps don't matter.

Example 2: Starting a career. This involves several steps: authentic self-knowledge, research into potential viable careers, deciding on a career, getting the right training, writing a winning resume, interviewing, and finding a good entry-level job that will help you advance. Each stage needs specific skill sets that should be considered separately. By breaking down the process, a person can analyze what areas need more development or knowledge so the entire set can work to propel them forward. And as with the first example, each of these big-picture stages can also be broken into smaller increments, too.

Let's go back to the assembly-line metaphor. Each stage's successful execution adds something else to the final product. Once you know the final product, you can ask your mentee to answer these questions.

1. How can I string successes together to create momentum?
2. How can I create intentionality around the concept so I can create momentum when it's needed?
3. How can I get "in the zone"?
4. When I'm "in the zone," how can I take advantage of it?

Stringing successful skills together is key to an excellence mindset. Not only does your young leader need to understand how to do individual tasks well; he or she also needs to understand how the whole process works together to establish a framework of greater excellence.

Your Misses Tell You What to Correct

Another concept Coach Pearson taught me that applies anywhere is something I've already mentioned: learning from your misses (mistakes) because they tell you what to correct.

"High jumpers" of all types—whether the bar they're shooting to clear is in a track meet or in a leadership setting—know that if they're working with me and they've "missed a jump," my first question is going to be, "What did that jump tell you?" "What did you do well?" and "What do you need to do better?"

After they've worked with me long enough, it's common for them to start answering those questions without my even asking them. I love that because it means they are internalizing their own evaluation and making themselves better.

As high jumpers, they learn how to read the signals. If their upper body hits the bar, they need to focus on planting their foot and driving to the sky. If their gluteus maximus region hits the bar, they need to focus on driving their hips to the sky, and if their legs or heels clip the bar, they need to focus on bringing their chin to their chest and kicking their feet. They must feel every aspect of the jump and translate their misses into successful later jumps.

This translates through to any setting. If you are reading the room and see frowns during your sales presentation, you haven't addressed a concern, or you've created another one you're not aware of. If you see people falling asleep, you're not engaging them enough. If you saw people smiling and nodding their heads during the pitch, but no one is returning your follow-up calls, you need to determine whether the decision makers have qualms. If your boss seems frustrated that you aren't responding to email fast enough, you need a new system for handling your email.

The earlier you can instill this process in your mentees, the better off they will be in analyzing and course correcting on their own—and their leaders and teammates will take notice of this and appreciate it. There's nothing better than a teammate who shows consistent initiative for improvement.

Beware of Dwelling on Mistakes

While it's good to be aware of mistakes, one danger of having a high standard is the tendency to dwell on them and obsess about how things "should have gone." If you or your Chosen gets into this mindset, beware! It's not productive. The rule for "criticism vs. constructive feedback" still applies—even when the criticism is internal.

When you allow your standards for excellence to outweigh everything else, you can lose sight of the bigger picture. In fact, this negative mindset can actually cause several other problems, such as sleep deprivation, mental illness, and a lack of innovative problem-solving, all of which can lead to making more mistakes![23]

Excellence doesn't mean perfection in every action—it means being extraordinary in the big picture. That requires accepting that there will be off days and that those can even indicate the need to adjust something so that the bigger picture doesn't suffer.

With Sarah in her high jump event, I could have focused on what she was doing wrong and told her to stop doing that—but that would just have held her attention on doing the wrong thing. It's a weird psychological effect, but whatever you put your attention on tends to get more important. If mistakes become super-important, they will sabotage your efforts.

For instance, suppose your mentee chooses to be extraordinary in every area in his/her life, and that means setting impossibly high standards for himself/herself and others. Eventually, meeting these standards causes your Chosen to get overly stressed and burn out. In addition, their super-high expectations of others result in being constantly disappointed in people for not meeting them.

With that mindset, your Chosen won't achieve long-term excellence in their mission areas because they'll erode their health and their ability to sustain such a focus. They'll also ruin the relationships that might otherwise help support them.

Be sure to remind your Chosen that mistakes are just learning opportunities, not measurements of a person's value. Risking new

---

23 A. Morin, "Science Says This Is What Happens to You When You Overthink Everything," *Inc.*, accessed March 10, 2022, https://www.inc.com/amy-morin/science-says-this-is-what-happens-when-you-overthink-things.html/.

things means making mistakes. If they fear making mistakes, they will actually stagnate their growth and learning.

Developing Confidence and Deploying Excellence

Developing excellence takes time—you know, about 10,000 hours—and that is where perseverance comes into the equation. Perseverance is the "continued effort to do or achieve something despite difficulties."[24] It may mean playing the same challenging piece of music thousands of times. Each time the musician plays it well, they build their confidence.

Confidence = excellent performance X times.

True confidence is rare in young athletes and leaders. As a society, we appreciate things that are convenient and efficient. We watch professional athletes and performers and think that we can be confident if we merely dress and act like them. We don't see the years of preparation that have gone into their excellent performance. All of the elements of developing excellence and confidence are neither convenient nor efficient.

As parents, we tend to want to rescue our children from difficulty. Out of love, we "clear the path" for the child or "grab the hammer" to do the job ourselves when we see them working hard or struggling with something new. I find avoiding this very difficult myself and have to bite my lip, resist "hammer grabbing," and learn to be patient. I know it's the best thing I can do for my growing leader, but it's really hard to watch them struggle. However, I find it reassuring that as I persist in the resistance to rescue that I, too, am developing true confidence in my parenting.

---

24 *Merriam-Webster Online Dictionary*, s.v. "perseverance (n.)," accessed April 30, 2022, https://www.merriam-webster.com/dictionary/perseverance/.

Part of building the "muscle" of excellence also involves testing. After hours of practice, the person must test the skill. Successfully passing the skills tests naturally builds true confidence. Testing the level of excellence in young leaders positions them to serve with excellence. Not only will the leader gain confidence, but you can deploy them confidently because you know they've passed their tests and are ready to meet the challenges.

Testing merely means deploying them while the "gutter guards" are still in place. Practice in a place where mistakes won't matter to test and refine skills until they are ready for the real arena. That means they need to be the ones using the hammer—and you have to stand back and let them hit their thumb a time or two to develop the right swing. (Though it's okay to have an ice pack handy, just in case.)

> *Confidence is a posture developed from numerous passed tests of excellence.*

If we resist rescuing them and allow our young leaders to grow true confidence, their display of it is a thing of beauty. You can generally tell by their genuine smile and bit of confident swagger. True confidence is a posture developed from numerous passed tests of excellence.

Exercise: Help Your Mentee Internalize Excellence and Gain Confidence

Chances are, if your mentee already has leadership qualities, they also already have a sense of excellence, even if they're not quite aware of or haven't fully developed it. Here's a way to get them thinking about this.

- Ask them to tell you a little about their most influential role models. Who has inspired them throughout their lives—was it a family member? A story they heard about a person who did something amazing? Someone they saw on television? Get them thinking.

- Ask them why those people influenced them. What was it about the person that struck them? How did the person behave? What did they accomplish in their lives? What obstacles did they face? How did they overcome them?
- Now ask them to think about what they would like to demonstrate as a role model themselves. How are they already showing a good example for others?
- You've already looked at their three dimensions of leadership (character, positive psychology, and soft skills) and determined the "holes" to plug. However, now let's look at the places where they're strongest. What led them to develop those areas more strongly? What values influenced and drove that self-development? Why did they already seek to be extraordinary in those areas?
- What about the idea of excellence motivates them? Is there anything about the idea of excellence that is daunting or scary? If so, why? What opportunities do they need to explore during their deployment phase that will help address those fears?
- What's the biggest mistake they've ever made? What did it teach them? How have they used that lesson to build more excellence in themselves? And if they haven't used it as a lesson, how could they do so now?
- Ask them to think about this and write a short paper about why, as a leader, they need to understand and demonstrate excellence. (Writing it makes them really think about it.) How will it help them in their career? Personal life? Relationships? How will not having it hinder them?

CHAPTER 8

Strategize

"I believe that people make their own luck by great preparation and good strategy."

—JACK CANFIELD

When you're deploying your Chosen, it's important to remain intentional. That means having a good strategy to make use of and build their skills, so they continue to gain confidence.

Whenever I think about strategy, I always think of the company Starbucks.

Steve Schulz didn't start the company. Three friends began it as a fun enterprise and a way to express their passion for great coffee. When they hired Schulz, they didn't know what they were in for.[25]

Schulz had a completely different idea about strategy than the original three. The store started out as a single retail venue where

---

25 Arthur Thompson, Jr. & A. J. Strickland "Starbucks Corporation," *Strategic Management: Concepts and Cases* (Burr Ridge, IL: McGraw-Hill, 1999), http://www.mhhe.com/business/management/thompson/11e/case/starbucks.html/.

people could buy coffee machines and beans to make their own coffee. But Schulz felt something was missing. He traveled to Italy and visited many of their local coffee shops—which the Italians call "bars." Yes, Italians are serious about their coffee.

Schulz came back with the idea to completely transform the entire enterprise by actually serving coffee on the premises. This didn't go over well with the owners, who wanted to do things the way they'd always been done. Even after Schulz tried serving coffee at one of the locations and had a line of waiting patrons that extended out the door and down the sidewalk, the three owners balked.

Eventually, Schulz left. He ended up starting his own company, Il Giornale, which eventually bought Starbucks and transformed it according to Schulz's strategy. The modest business took off, becoming today's global enterprise with a Starbucks seemingly on every corner. Schulz's strategy was clear: make the coffee shop a place to gather during the day (as opposed to an alcohol bar at night) and enjoy good conversation and coffee. Equipment sales were not the key—Starbucks would make the coffee for its customers. It was about atmosphere and ambience, not just a cheap cup of coffee. In fact, the coffee was not cheap at all. Yet people paid for it because Schulz had hit on something. Apparently, people wanted this new kind of experience. Even going through the drive-through was a brief encounter with this brand that imparted the sense that there was a friendly place to go and hang out, even if they could only briefly touch on it via their car for a moment and carry the coffee on their way.

Schulz developed his strategy because he saw a need and wanted to fill it. He had a vision fueled by caffeine, yes, but mainly by his own positive experience in many friendly, welcoming coffee bars in Italy. Why couldn't America have such places? His goal was clear—and the rest was history.

Strategy Creates Opportunity

Don't let this story intimidate you—I don't expect you to create a global coffee retailer. But it doesn't hurt to think like a top-level CEO for just a few minutes and use strategy when deploying your Chosen.

Excellent leaders serve at deep, meaningful levels with maximum impact. A strategy allows them to intentionally align their values and skills to give the highest levels of service. It allows them to deploy their potential in ways that bring the greatest value. Strategy enables the young leader to prioritize their focus where it will count most and leave other things to other people who can do them better.

> *Leaders serve at deep, meaningful levels with maximum impact.*

Schulz didn't try to make Starbucks a better coffee equipment and bean retailer because he didn't see the vision within that strategy. It didn't resonate with him. It was fun for the owners and their regular customers, but Schulz saw more to be done. He wasn't "right," and the original owners weren't "wrong," either. Both groups just had different focus areas and visions. The original owners were happy in their business, regardless of whether it went global. In fact, you could argue that they were probably happier when it wasn't global. Their particular skills and vision didn't include a global vision.

Schulz didn't settle for their vision and try to make it work—he moved on, only to later find himself back again, in a different capacity. Had he merely settled for someone else's choices for how he should operate, the world would not have thousands of Starbucks shops with the scent of caramel latte wafting out to entice people on sidewalks to come in and enjoy a quick break.

That's why strategy has to resonate with your Chosen, or it won't work. It has to be driven by their goals, talents, and passions—not yours. When they're contributing in their true, mission-oriented way, they can accomplish amazing things.

Early in my kids' schooling years, I remember having a conversation with their principal. It started something like this, "I don't want to bake cookies, but if you really need some, I'll bring them." My statement got his attention. He paused for a moment, then asked, "In what other ways would you like to be involved?" We had a delightful conversation, and I went on to explain that I wanted to use my skills in a meaningful way to help the school.

In my career, I have led multiple selection committees, served as a classroom teacher and coach, designed curricula, and mentored young professionals. I wanted to serve in similar ways with my kids' school as needed. I didn't mind baking a few cookies, but I didn't *only* want to bake cookies. I felt I could make a deeper impact if my skill set was known and used strategically.

We went on to have a great relationship for many years, and now my "strategic" service has carried on to middle school and high school. Sure, I've baked some cookies—but not only that, I have been blessed to serve our school corporation on the calendaring committee and as part of a selection committee for a new principal. My authentic understanding of myself allowed me to create more opportunities for contributions in areas where I could make a greater impact.

Your young leader is going to encounter situations where they, like Schulz as a business strategist or me as a parent, have to choose how they want to be involved. Teach them to think strategically about how they invest their time. If they only have time to do one thing, what's most important for the organization, and how does that intersect with their passions, skills, and knowledge? What kind of skill, knowledge, and passion does it involve?

If it's a skill that aligns with their values directly and also builds important relationships over time, that's a strategic deployment. There's nothing inherently "wrong" with selling coffee equipment. If that's their passion, why not do it? And there's nothing wrong with baking cookies, either. If they're passionate about cookies or baking in general, baking cookies would be a key alignment! It just wasn't one of *my* key alignments.

Deployment Strategy vs. Development Plan

Before we go any further, let's make some clarifications between the action plan for development and their strategy for deployment. Both involve planning and are related, but they have different sets of goals.

The development plan is the way in which they focus on how they can improve their skills and leadership dimensions to achieve a specific goal within a specific timeframe. A deployment strategy, on the other hand, is a long-term strategy for how they want to shape their career and general life around their values and mission, deploying their skills over time while still learning and growing. The development plan is about what they will develop in themselves; the deployment strategy is about how they will bring those newly developed elements to the world in their own unique way.

Start with Their Values

A leader's values should serve as their North Star in the development of their leadership strategy. Values aligning with service is the first step in making maximum impact.

Howard Schulz's values lay in creating cozy neighborhood retreats, where people could have friendly conversations with their local barista and catch up on all the latest happenings. It was another version of the local bar, only with coffee. He was passionate about that vision and could translate it into everything about Starbucks, even down to the carefully calculated brand colors, the smell of coffee roasting in the shop, and other aspects. He didn't want to sell coffee. He wanted to create a culture around coffee—one that was welcoming and enjoyable.

Dolly Parton is another prime example of values-driven leadership. Her iconic voice has made us come to know her, but many have fallen in love with Dolly because of her philanthropy, which has been spotlighted over the past few years. Though Dolly has earned fifty Grammy Awards, has a theme park named after her, and has written more than three thousand songs over the span of her fifty-year career, her humble beginnings and desire to help unfortunate communities have shaped her into a humanitarian icon.

In 1995, Dolly launched a program called Dolly Parton's Imagination Library to promote literacy among children in Tennessee, and the program has now expanded worldwide. After the 2016 wildfires in East Tennessee, Dolly held a telethon that raised $413 million for residents in the region. And most recently, Dolly announced that she would donate $1 million to the Vanderbilt University Medical Center to aid its research efforts.

"Dolly grew up in Sevier County, Tennessee, one of the poorest counties in the country," wrote Ellie Selden of *The Duke Chronicle*. "As she rose to fame and wealth, her past economic struggles humbled her, leading to a philanthropic journey that has persisted throughout her career. She has certainly aligned her values with her service for maximum impact."[26]

So, let's go back to your Chosen's values, which you should already be very familiar with if you've followed along in the stages of this book. Starting from there, we can create a model for strategizing their deployment.

The T Model

The T-shaped Professional Model or T-shaped person is a reference to qualities that make a professional valuable.

The top of the T represents a breadth of knowledge and the ability to apply knowledge across situations. Breadth of knowledge just refers to general, big-picture knowledge across a wide variety of subjects related to the area of main focus. The leg of the T represents deep expertise in specific functional and disciplinary skills related to the area of main focus.

To succeed, a professional must have both a breadth and depth of knowledge of their discipline. They must understand enough about the broader, more general areas to comprehend and respond to their general situations, while also having a deep functional knowledge and specific skills within their discipline. All these qualities combine to make them an expert at something specific or some sets of specific things within the general area of focus.

---

26 Ellie Selden, "A Look Back at Dolly Parton's Philanthropic Legacy," *The Duke Chronicle*, March 4, 2021, https://www.dukechronicle.com/article/2021/03/dolly-parton-philanthropy-vaccine-dollywood-foundation/.

T Model for Strategic Leadership Deployment

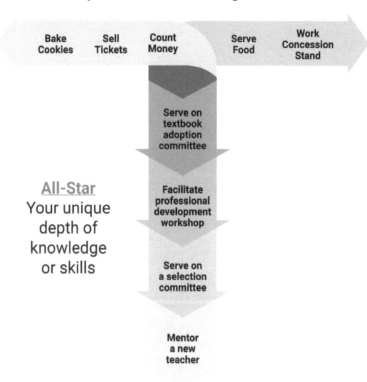

Using the T Model in Leadership Deployment

The T model is helpful when determining a strategy for deploying leadership. The question is, "where can they make maximum impact?' Many times, depth is the place of greatest impact.

For example, going back to my own story of the cookies, I could bake cookies, take tickets, count money, and serve drinks. I am happy to apply my breadth of knowledge in these areas as needed.

But my *depth* of knowledge and skills in education also allow me to serve in a deeper, more meaningful way. I was able to communicate my skills to the principal, and when he had an opening that matched my skill set, he knew whom to call. It was a win-win situation.

Value-driven service and knowledge of the T model have been game-changers for me. They serve as a guide that allows me to confidently and willingly serve in meaningful, deep ways with maximum impact. They also allow me to assertively say no to areas of service that don't align well and open the door to communicate ways I would like to serve.

The sooner emerging leaders understand this strategy in deploying what they're learning and their leadership in general, the sooner they will be able to make maximum impact without getting off track. As mentors, let's bolster them with this knowledge early in their careers so they can start stronger, go further faster, and have maximum impact in our world!

The Other Side of the Equation: Needs

As you consider the types of skills and knowledge your Chosen is going to demonstrate, you need the other component: what does the situation require?

If you're looking at deployment within an organization, what is that organization looking for?

If you're looking at deployment in a general field to determine the best career options, what is that field lacking? What challenges are those within it facing that need to be overcome? These are questions to ask your mentee.

When to Ask for More Help

In my situation with the Krannert student leadership organization, when I deployed certain students, I did so with the need in mind. Obviously, I had a deep knowledge of that because it was within my area of responsibility. I could clearly identify and articulate the need.

When you're coaching or mentoring others within your own field, you probably already understand most of the general challenges that field is facing at the time, and you're probably naturally looking for people who can meet those challenges. You're a good source of information in that respect, though you might call in others to give supplemental help where needed.

However, when you're mentoring someone in a more general way, such as helping a young person decide on a career or solve some other general problem, you may not know all the specifics of the situation they would need to be aware of—nor should you be expected to. It's not your area of expertise.

As a coach or mentor, your role is to guide and provide resources where applicable. You don't have to be the only one helping your mentee. Sometimes that means asking for help from an expert in another area your mentee needs to explore. In those cases, don't try to get the information yourself. Just ask your contact for permission to refer the mentee and let them figure out their specific plan for that step. You don't have to be directly involved. You're just there to provide potential resources and guidance where it makes sense for you to do so. Your mentee needs to be ready to do some additional work to answer his or her own questions and fill in knowledge gaps.

Exercise: Do a T Model for Your Chosen

Now it's your turn. Working with your Chosen, complete the T model with the information relevant to them and their own strategic focus. This will help them make decisions about how and where to deploy their skills for the biggest impact.

T Model for Strategic Leadership Deployment

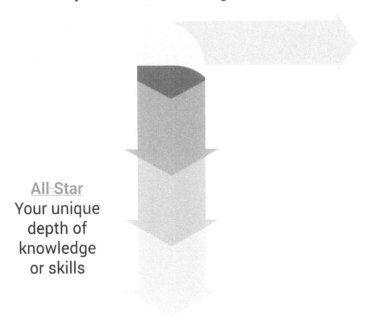

Average
Fairly Common Knowledge or Skills

All-Star
Your unique depth of knowledge or skills

CHAPTER 9

Adapt

"Agility within and of itself is a strategy."
—PEARL ZHU

In the military, strategy isn't optional. It saves lives and wins battles.

But nobody knows better than the military that strategy itself can be a moving target.

My friend, Steve Taylor, is a retired major with the National Guard and a former army ranger. He has a combined thirty-four years of military operations experience, which he carried on into leadership roles in the private sector.

When Steve was an army ranger, his battalion was part of Operation Just Cause, the 1989 mission to overthrow the infamous Panama drug trafficker and dictator, Manuel Noriega.

Army command wanted everything done right the first time. "They didn't want to do any preemptive strikes, so they were accepting up to 60 percent casualties on the initial assault," he said. "We knew we had to play it to a T. We didn't have much room for error."

At 1:30 a.m. on December 20, parachute troops conducted an assault on Panama. Their goal was to jump into specific points, taking strategic assets into enemy territory to gain control.

Steve recalled the story of one 18- or 19-year-old private, who had only been in the army for six months. The private was an assistant gunner for an anti-tank weapons system. His job was to parachute in carrying a big infrared scope that was part of the weapons system.

"It was pretty rocky as we were going in; the plane was getting shot up pretty badly," Steve recalled. "As he was trying to jump, he got stuck—tripped and fell. But the plane kept flying."

The young gunner finally got up to the door, but since he was so late, it was up to him whether to go or not—two miles past the drop zone.

He decided to jump.

Landing, he found himself approximately two miles out in the middle of the jungle by himself, at night, with no idea where his unit was.

However, he quickly realized he wasn't by himself.

"This young guy gets the scope out and is looking, and all of a sudden this huge spotlight shines out of the sky and floods the whole area," Steve recalled.

Feeling a moment of terror at being totally exposed, the young private put the scope down—and suddenly, there was no spotlight.

His mind working quickly, the young private began to recall his training. "Rangers were big on the fact that whatever we would do, we would rehearse it," Steve said. "Every person had to know the plan from start to finish—they had to understand the running passwords, know the locations of each unit in case they got outside the wire."

The young gunner realized that the spotlight was an infrared spotlight—one of the Army's Spectre assets. He could only see it through the scope he carried. "Spectre had weapons systems, but part of it was a regular spotlight, and another part was an infrared spotlight," Steve explained. "The infrared looks just like a regular spotlight shining down when you're looking through night vision glasses, but with the naked eye, you can't see anything."

The young private saw through the scope that the infrared spotlight was moving and then would come back to him. He suddenly realized what was going on—his air support was using the spotlight to guide him back to his unit.

He also had additional help figuring out where he was. As part of the plan, the planes flew at 360 degrees, becoming a quick reference for the jumpers to get their bearings in the confusing jungle terrain. "The wind takes you all over the place," Steve said. "It's easy to get confused."

Steve himself, as Forward Observer, had had to brief everyone in his platoon on the plan and all of these assets. He had given the paratroopers a quick lesson on what to do if they had to call in for help. Recalling the vital information, the private quickly recovered his bearings. Spectre guided him through unfamiliar territory and even around enemy troops, keeping him out of trouble until, with only a couple hours' delay, he linked up with his unit, uninjured, to deliver the infrared scope he was carrying.

Adapting on the Fly

Having a plan is important—but the most important part is that everyone knows and follows through with achieving the ultimate goal. In the military, Steve explained, this is known as the "commander's intent."

The commander can't make all the decisions, but if people on the floor know the intent, they can make their own decisions on the fly as they encounter unexpected circumstances.

And unexpected circumstances are bound to happen. Steve notes that they have a joke that's actually a truth: "The enemy has a vote, too." Things will change. If the enemy suspects the plan, they aren't going to willingly go along with it—in fact, they'll do just the opposite. The plan has to include response to unexpected conditions.

Also, other things happen that are out of the planners' control—weather, human error, and other things that can't be predicted individually.

The trick isn't to try to predict every possible contingency—it's to have a framework that enables better decisions, to communicate it solidly, and to ensure everyone knows the ultimate goal, as well as their individual goals and how everything fits within the framework, so they can make their own decisions when needed. Keeping the end goal in mind makes decisions much easier.

Agility on a Grander Leadership Scale

Being able to think quickly and adapt to changing circumstances is the mark of agility—and it's a vital skill for both you and your Chosen as they deploy their leadership skills.

While agility at a corporate level might not be as lifesaving as in the military, senior executives rank it at the top of the leadership capabilities needed for business success.[27]

---

27 Bill Joiner, "Duke: The Leadership Ability Factor," Duke Corporate, December 2013.

But what exactly is leadership agility, and how do leaders put it into practice?

At its core, leadership agility is the ability to take "reflective action,"—to step back from one's current focus, gain a broader, deeper perspective, then refocus and take action that is informed by this larger perspective. As emerging leaders become more agile, their capacity to gain a broader, deeper perspective grows, and their leadership action increases.

> *As emerging leaders become more agile, their capacity to gain a broader, deeper perspective grows, and their leadership action increases.*

Why Young Leaders Need Agility

Agility manifests in multiple areas:

- **Emotional agility**—the ability to quickly understand and control their emotional responses and direct them to positive outcomes.

- **Technical agility**—the ability to adapt skills to new situations or quickly learn new skills where needed.

- **Mental agility**—the ability to consciously shift their thinking, perspectives, and application when and how the situation requires it (agile thinking).

The preceding abilities give young leaders multiple advantages when making decisions and adapting to new circumstances. In other words, they'll be able to start stronger and go further faster.

It's the difference between a traditional catapult and an accelerator. Traditionally, a catapult is used to throw an object over a distance. On an aircraft carrier, the planes must take off with a very limited amount of space. Therefore, the carrier uses a type of catapult called an accelerator to boost the aircraft's speed during takeoff so that it can get fully airborne using the minimum amount of distance. When you're deploying your Chosen, you want to give them the equivalent of an accelerator to get them moving quickly.

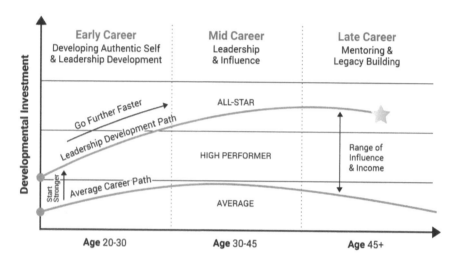

The Key to Agility

You'll notice that the preceding areas where agility manifests strongly reflect the leadership dimensions of character, power skills, and positive psychology—the "three spheres." That's not an accident.

The key to agility begins with one simple thing: authentic self-knowledge. When your Chosen know themselves and have developed true confidence in the areas of power skills, positive psychology, and character, their decision-making becomes much easier. They've already strategized how they will deploy themselves to fulfill their mission. They've already been taught to think strategically in general. They know what and how to prioritize.

Due to their self-knowledge and the practice and thought they've already put in during the preceding stages of mentorship, they'll have more confidence about decisions in general. Their preparation will boost their ability to assess midstream and alter course more quickly to meet organizational goals. They will know their ability and where they bring value, and they will be able to assess situations and projects and make adjustments when necessary. They will also be able to assess others in this way, quickly determining how to assign work and determine other roles based on their teams' strengths to obtain maximum results.

Self-Leadership

Remember how we discussed your Chosen internalizing the definitions and examples of excellence for themselves so that they could make their own decisions on how to define and expect them of themselves? That's a facet of self-leadership—the ability for leaders to understand and lead themselves. Self-leadership happens to be a dimension of leadership agility.

Even if they don't begin with strong self-knowledge, it's a skill that, like any other, can be developed. Here's a way you can assess where your Chosen is in this area.

Self-leadership involves three core competencies. According to Andrew Bryant:

1. **Self-awareness** is the individual's tendency to focus on and reflect on their own mental processes and inner experiences as well as their relationships to others.

2. **Self-learning** is the process by which individuals take initiative to identify their own learning needs, goals, resources, and outcomes.

3. **Self-regulation** is the way an individual balances attention, emotion, and behavior regarding a given situation/stimulus, so as to pursue a goal.[28]

Agility means the ability to adjust as we learn more about ourselves. As with Steve's story, the plan is only as good as the first thing that goes wrong. After that, the goal drives the adjustments to the plan.

Your Chosen has worked to instill his or her own "commander's intent" throughout this process of development. How does that guide them when things don't go as planned or when they discover something new about themselves that requires a change?

For instance, my own career has taken several turns. I didn't start out deciding I was going to be where I am today, with my own coaching business. But I do remember the beautiful spring morning when I was called into student development and coaching. I was on campus at Ball State University for my in-person interview for graduate school admittance. Of course, I was a bit nervous entering the main administration building for the interview, but I had nothing to lose. My interview went well, and I actually enjoyed it. As I exited, I glanced back at the building, and time somewhat stood still. The building was glowing in the sunshine, and my soul was glowing as well, knowing that I had just hit upon my life's calling. That picture and feeling will be seared into my memory forever.

Throughout my life, I have taken several positions that built on different facets of this calling—which served as my "commander's intent." Within each, I learned new things and developed my skills

---

28 Andrew Bryant Self-Leadership, "Measuring Self-Leadership: the Future of Work," August 25, 2021, https://www.selfleadership.com/blog/measuring-self-leadership-profiling-situational-judgment-test

in ways that I would never have expected when standing in front of that building so long ago. Like the spotlight guiding the young gunner back to his unit, my goal of helping develop young leaders has guided me through every decision and challenge, always bringing me back to my original calling—just in a new way.

Your Chosen can't create a strategy and expect everything to go perfectly and seamlessly until they arrive, pristine and right on time, at their desired destination. The world just doesn't work that way.

You and your Chosen also can't expect that their knowledge, skills, drives, passions, and needs will remain static. They have to respond to both inner and outer changes throughout their lives. The earlier they start realizing how to do that, the better off they'll be.

Exercise: Be an Example of Agility

Reflect on your own life and career, and then answer the following questions.

1. How have you shown agility in your decisions?

2. Where did you make your mistakes? What did you learn from them?

3. How can your experience be an example of agility for your Chosen?

4. Are there others you can point them to as well to help them see how to develop their own agility?

CHAPTER 10

What's Next?

"…Stop waiting for someone to make your life count. You need to act. You need to act as if your life depends on it, because it does. Life is action. Only the dead stay still."

—ERWIN RAPHAEL MCMANUS, THE LAST ARROW

Now that you have the tools to mentor more effectively, you can deploy them to find more mentees and continue practicing and improving your skills. (Remember: Discover, Develop, Deploy, and repeat.) The result of seeing your Chosen move out to make their places in the world and bring their skills to solve the problems of tomorrow will be a great reward in itself, but there's even more.

Because they will also go out and mentor others, who will mentor others…into infinity.

The ripple effect of this could be world-changing—and that's my hope. I would like nothing more than to see an entire community of people-minded mentors, all sharing their ideas and tips with each other to make the world a better place.

It's Time to Act

If you've read this book through without acting on any of it yet, I get it. You want to test the waters before you jump headfirst into the pool. That makes sense. Most people like to know what they're getting into before taking action.

But if you're about to put this book on a shelf or in a corner somewhere where it will sit forgotten, gathering dust, I implore you to pause and think about one last thing: your potential Chosen. They're waiting for someone, anyone, to take an interest in them and help them get on the best path for themselves.

They're waiting for someone to notice them and tell them that they just might be the next extraordinary leader who will do something amazing for the world.

They're waiting for you.

They've already been waiting years. Please don't make them wait any longer. It's too easy for tomorrow to become next month, which becomes next year…and suddenly, ten years have gone by with no action.

You know that old saying, it takes a village to raise a child? It applies to leaders, too. It takes a community of leaders to lift up the new ones, speak life into them, and give them the guidance they need. If we don't do that, we can't complain when we get to the stage where we're ready to pass the baton to the next generation…and find there's no one there who knows how to take it and run with it. What would that kind of world look like?

I don't want to find out. And I'm betting you don't, either. Let's not let that happen.

My biggest hope is that this book will be like a stone I'm throwing into a still pond—and that it brings the first ripple of many. Let's try for ripples that will spread across not only the country, but the world. Even if we don't achieve that, we'll have achieved something important. But if we do achieve that—if enough people take action—the ripples will become waves, and there's no telling what will happen.

But we do know one thing: it will be extraordinary.

Circle of Impact

As you're contemplating the shift of your mentoring relationship to a relationship between two peers instead, it's time to ask your Chosen a question.

Who have they observed who needs a good mentor? Who can they put on their own bucket list?

Yes, I see you grinning.

But we have to get the next ripple moving, don't we?

Most likely, they'll already be thinking along those lines. According to PushFar, 90 percent of young adults with a mentor are interested in becoming one in the future.[29]

But if they are concerned about whether they have what it takes or don't know where to begin, you can just hand them a copy of this book. It can be a parting gift to show them they've reached the stage where you're confident they are ready to start serving others in this way, too.

Don't get me wrong: I'm not in this to sell more books. I'm in this to make more mentors. That's my mission. It's why I wrote this book. It's what drives me every day. It's what fuels my passion for success. Success, to me, amounts to that community of mentors—extraordinary people all working together to help others achieve

---

[29] PushFar, April, 2022.

extraordinary things, too. If you're reading this, you have selected yourself to be in that community, and I welcome you wholeheartedly! And I'm ready to welcome your Chosen, too—we just have to get them to that point.

I suspect that if your Chosen are strong leaders, they'll be as excited as you and I are about helping others. After all, we're here to solve problems and serve people, right? Isn't helping grow new leaders who will go out and do awesome things one of the best ways to do that? We can't do this thing all by ourselves. We're all part of a circle of impact. Every person has something to offer.

That includes you—and all your Chosen.

I wish you the best in your adventures together, and I look forward to hearing about them.

The Starfish Story

One day a man was walking along the beach when he noticed a boy picking something up and gently throwing it into the ocean.

Approaching the boy, he asked, "What are you doing?"

The youth replied, "Throwing starfish back into the ocean. The surf is up, and the tide is going out. If I don't throw them back, they'll die."

"Son," the man said, "don't you realize there are miles and miles of beach and hundreds of starfish? You can't make a difference!"

After listening politely, the boy bent down, picked up another starfish, and threw it back into the surf. Then, smiling at the man, he said," I made a difference for that one."

—Original story by Loren Eisely

Thank You

"Your ideas will change, your challenges will change, the world will change, but when you know who is with you and you know who you are with, you can face whatever is yet to come."

—ERWIN RAPHAEL MCMANUS, THE LAST ARROW

Thank you for reading *Average to All-Star*. Your time and attention are a gift, and I appreciate your allowing me to share my thoughts on how you can speak life into others.

I am deeply grateful to my colleagues, students, friends, and family who have encouraged me to share my experiences and expertise. They have shaped my understanding of developing others. Thank you to the many individuals who shared their stories in an effort to positively impact others.

Please share this book with others—leaders, students of leadership, those you want to encourage, those who have impact, and your Chosen. My profound wish is that this book helps build healthy leaders of tomorrow and a community of mentors to develop and support them.

I'd love to hear your thoughts about the book, and especially what it has sparked in others through you. Write an online review, send a personal note, or pick up the phone and call me. Your "light-bulb" moments of insight, your suggestions for improvement, and your thoughts on how to impact our future leaders are all helpful in creating our community of mentors.

It is my sincere hope that you will choose to invest in many emerging leaders so they can start strong and go further faster in their lives. Thanks for being with me in this mission.

Onward and upward!
Sharlee

About the Author

Sharlee Lyons is a multi-dimensional professional whose entire career has focused on developing others. A former Division 1 athlete, Sharlee brought her love of leadership coaching to the corporate, non-profit, and higher education sectors, serving for more than twenty years as an expert in developing authentic emerging leaders and leadership teams.

She is a certified Gallup Strengths Coach, a Master Consultant with Growing Leaders, a Fascinate Certified Advisor, and an accredited coach by the International Coaching Federation. Now, through The People Business, Sharlee serves as a speaker, teacher, coach, and consultant with a passion for working with individuals and teams to develop future leaders in all settings.

Sharlee and her husband, Todd, live in Lafayette, Indiana, with their two teenagers, Noah and Sarah, who serve as the test market for all her training content, and whom she feels demonstrate some of her best work.

Contact Sharlee

For speaking engagements, coaching, workshops, or leadership development consulting, contact Sharlee at:

Website: SharleeLyons.com
Email: sharlee@sharleelyons.com
LinkedIn: linkedin.com/in/sharlee-lyons-m-a-37b0ba16

Download Sharlee's Coaching and Mentoring Toolkit!
SharleeLyons.com/toolkit